# CLEAR, CONCISE & COMPELLING

## How to Present to Change Minds and Influence Outcomes

For Theresa,

Because so much of life success is about being clear, concise and compelling!

Cheers!

Susan

# CLEAR, CONCISE & COMPELLING

## How to Present to Change Minds and Influence Outcomes

**SUSAN GARRITY BISH**

AUTHOR
ACADEMY elite

Printed in the United States of America

Published by Author Academy Elite
PO Box 43, Powell, OH 43035
www.AuthorAcademyElite.com

Identifiers: LCCN: 2019907341
ISBN: 978-1-64085-729-2 (paperback)
ISBN: 978-1-64085-730-8 (hardback)
ISBN: 978-1-64085-731-5 (ebook)

Available in paperback, hardback, e-book, and audiobook

This book is dedicated to the people in my life who made it possible:

My husband and business partner, Myron, whose ever-present support and continuous improvement mentality helped create our presentation skills workshop and this book

My sons Colin, Kevin and Chris who inspire me daily to pursue new goals

My parents, Pat and Bill Garrity, who encouraged me to embrace life fully

My clients, who eagerly embrace the Clear, Concise & Compelling skills and prove that being an influential presenter changes careers

# CONTENTS

# CHAPTER 1

# The Journey to Great Presentations

## Lessons from Wine Tasting

"So, it's settled. We're off to northern California for three days of wine tasting! Thanks for being our tour guides." Somehow an evening out with two couples ended up with my husband and me in charge of a long weekend getaway. Not that we objected. We've visited the wine country many times; it's one of our favorite things to do. And we were looking forward to sharing some favorite wineries with our friends.

The planning process was fun. We made a list of our favorite places. Then we visited websites to explore additional vintners to add to our list. Because we only had three days, we planned on visiting seven wineries each day. After much deliberation, we narrowed the list to 21 wineries in the Sonoma region. Because our friends indicated they wanted to learn about winemaking, we also booked two stops with behind-the-scenes private tours focused exclusively on that craft.

Next, we mapped out each day to make sure we made the best use of time. We did our homework, picked two exceptional restaurants and made reservations for the evenings we'd be there. After probably 30 hours of research and planning, it all came together. We even created an itinerary for each day with timing and information about each stop.

Day one was amazing. A beautiful northern California experience. The first three stops were right on schedule. The first behind-the-scenes tour was incredible with respect to the level of information we picked up. But then we started falling behind. Lunch took longer than expected. And the hosts at the tasting bars of the next two wineries were so engaging that it was four o'clock before we knew it. Our group decided they were done for the day.

That created a bit of a dilemma. Do we change our itinerary for the next two days to fit in the two places we missed on day one? We decided to ditch those and do better at staying on schedule on day two.

No such luck. We accomplished our morning plan, hitting three terrific wineries. After lunch we made two more stops. But by midafternoon, our group was ready to relax by the pool.

On day three, we made it to only four of the seven wineries. As we sat in the airport waiting for our flight, we reflected on our wine getaway. While everyone loved the wineries we visited, we all agreed we tried to do too much in too little time. The group also decided that for the next trip, we needed to factor in time to enjoy some hiking and resting and spend a little less time on wine.

Why didn't all of our research and planning result in a perfect vacation? What went wrong? It turns out the focus of our trip was off. We didn't do a good job of identifying exactly what our group wanted to accomplish on the trip and tried to do too much. We thought it was all about learning as much as possible about wine. In reality, we didn't understand what they wanted to do. Our friends were more interested in a relaxing weekend with some great winery experiences rather than a weekend overstuffed with learning. We also learned that the in-depth private tours were way more than our friends wanted or needed. While they were great, our friends did not find it a good use of time.

So, my husband and I made a few notes to guide our planning for future trips:

- What do our travel companions want to make it an unforgettable trip?

- What experiences does our group want to have?

- How much do they know about wine?

- What do they want to learn?

- What will contribute to them raving about the trip when they return?

- What are their limitations? What would be too much?

As I reflected on what we learned from taking our friends on this trip, it occurred to me that leading a group on a journey is quite similar to what I teach clients about designing and delivering effective presentations.

## An influential journey

Like a journey, good presentations are intended to accomplish something: provide new information to change thinking, get a commitment, secure a decision, obtain support or close a deal. Presentations are primarily about influence—defined as the power to change or affect someone or something without directly forcing it to happen. The presenter's goal is to influence an outcome. To achieve this, you must...

- *Be clear:* Know exactly where you want to take the audience—your influence objective

- *Be concise:* Include only as much information as necessary

- *Be compelling:* Understand the needs of the audience—why will they go on this journey with you?

Let's take a quick look at each of these.

## Be clear: Know exactly where you want to take the audience

Every presentation is an opportunity to take your audience with you to a specific destination. On our wine trip, we needed to narrow down the destination from learning about wine tasting to having a fun and relaxing weekend with friends that included wine tasting.

What is it that you want the audience to know, feel and do as a result of attending your presentation? What is the *why* of your presentation? It is important to be specific about this destination. Unfortunately, many presentations are more focused on the *what*. Average presenters do not have a specific influence objective for their presentations. Great presenters, on the other hand, design their entire presentation to accomplish their influence objective—it is made clear in the introduction, supported by foundational points in the body and driven home in the conclusion.

## Include only as much information as necessary

In hindsight, it was easy to see that fewer wineries would have been a better design for our trip. Great presenters are careful not to present extraneous information. They present the right content in the right amount. They don't try to do too much.

The digital age is exploding with information. Because it is so easily accessible, it is tempting to include too much. Your challenge when designing a presentation is to determine what to include—and what to leave out. Average presenters overstuff their presentations with too much information. This leaves the audience wondering what is most important. Great presenters know that less is definitely more and better when it comes to presenting influentially.

## Understand the needs of the audience

On our wine trip, had we taken the time to understand what our friends already knew and what they wanted to learn about wine, we would have designed a very different experience! We needed to ask better questions.

People who attend a presentation usually do so because they need something. They are looking to solve a problem, identify an opportunity or confirm their beliefs. Great presenters take the time and do the research to understand what the audience needs and wants relative to the presentation topic. They present in a way that reaches the audience by helping them solve their problem, understand your opportunity or provide evidence that confirms their beliefs.

## Be clear, concise and compelling on purpose

Think about the last presentation you attended (or gave) that was only okay. Chances are that one or more of the following conditions existed:

- The presenter lacked a specific objective
- The presentation did not meet the needs of the audience
- The presenter tried to do too much and included too much information

All too often in presentations like these, the presenter misses the opportunity to help the audience take away something useful, and also misses the chance to be memorable for all the right reasons.

The good news is that everyone from nervous introverts to overpowering extroverts can develop influential presentation skills. Our workshop participants have proven year after year that these skills are learnable. We've seen incredible skill development with novices and seasoned presenters and entry-level to C suite professionals in marketing, sales, science, engineering and many other functions. This book distills down our experience into actionable steps that can transform anyone into a great presenter.

## Strong presentation skills can lead to career success

The Center for Creative Leadership identifies *influencing others* as one of the four core leadership skills needed for success. "Without the capacity to influence others, your ability to make what you envision a reality remains elusive." And presentations are one of the most common and effective ways to influence.

My company, Bottom Line Technologies, exists to help individuals develop the skills they need for career success. About twenty years ago, we had a thought-provoking conversation with a highly respected client. She identified that many of the top performers in her company did not get the respect they deserved because they appeared average when presenting. Lack of competence, nervousness and obvious lack of confidence prevented these individuals from shining. She asked if we could help. This was the beginning of our journey in designing our influential presentation skills workshop.

I could certainly relate to my client's observations. Early in my corporate career I noticed that many company "stars" were great presenters. In some cases, they were better at presenting than they were in completing job responsibilities. One individual comes to mind. Sarah was ten years into her career and on the fast track. She was a competent product manager but a brilliant presenter. People looked forward to her presentations. She was engaging, compelling, logical and an excellent storyteller. Because she delivered presentations with poise and polish, she gained respect—perhaps even more than her job performance deserved. Yet she advanced to the vice president level quickly.

Through the years, I've heard many similar stories of how excellent presentation skills have helped people advance in their careers. I've also had individuals tell me they feel as though their lack of presentation skills has held them back.

Our influential presentation skills workshops, distilled down to the following chapters, provide the techniques to help presenters eliminate the things that get in the way and strengthen those that make for a great presentation.

## What makes a presentation great

In developing our workshop, we started by exploring what makes a great presentation great. That list included the obvious: strong delivery, interesting content, ability to hold attention. We also looked at the common pitfalls that make presentations ineffective. You can easily guess what made this list: dull, dry, boring, over-stuffed, rambling and the lack of a clear presentation objective. There are two major components to a presentation that can make or break your attempt to influence your audience: the content and the delivery.

The content—everything from the structure and organization to slide design to what you include and exclude—can carefully guide an audience to reach your desired conclusion. Poor content fails to engage the audience, loses them in the wilderness of a meandering story or complicated spreadsheet, even literally puts them to sleep.

Many presenters invest a disproportionate amount of time and energy into packing slides full of information, and far too little in thinking about an objective, the expectations of the audience and how to make the key points of the presentation stick.

Weak delivery skills also challenge many presenters. You've probably seen all of these behaviors in presenters: a monotone voice, use of filler words, weak eye contact, random movements, lack of positive gestures, low energy, no smile. In contrast, a strong presenter has good voice modulation and a dynamic energy in front of the room that engages the audience without overpowering. These skills are not only the natural gifts of a lucky few; they can be learned and honed with practice.

In short: clear, concise and compelling. These are the key elements that take a presentation from painful to passable to great. The following chapters will help you create a presentation with these three concepts at the forefront, from planning to slide preparation to presentation day.

## Why this book?

I was fortunate to have received presentation skills training early in my career, and I'm passionate about helping others build the skills they need to succeed. I love seeing workshop participants become competent and confident in delivering influential presentations. That's why I've written this book—it contains the tools, techniques and tips we deliver in our two-day workshops so that you can present influentially.

This book is unique because you can apply these skills immediately. It provides the *how*, not just the what and why. It is intended to serve as a resource you can return to for every presentation. Each chapter identifies specific things you can do to influence the audience. At the end of each chapter you will find ideas on how to put the content to work. Dive into the specific chapter where you need the most help or continue reading from here to the end of the book. This is what we will cover:

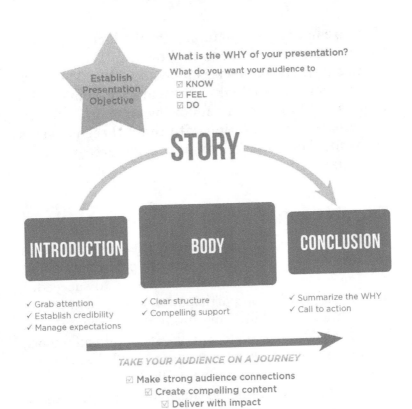

## Chapter 2    Establish Your Objective

Learn to be specific about what you want to accomplish with each presentation. What is the *why* of your presentation? Be specific, clear and concise about what you want the audience to know, feel and do. Plan to take your audience on a journey. What's your destination? Why will people go there with you?

## Chapter 3    Make a Strong Audience Connection

Connect logically, emotionally and memorably with your audience so they will take this journey with you. Do your homework to ensure you know what the audience knows about your topic and what they need to know. How does the audience make decisions? Learn what influence levers will work best for each audience. Only when you understand your audience and their needs can you create and deliver a presentation that will be compelling.

## Chapter 4    Create Compelling Content

Influential content starts with a solid presentation structure. You must create and deliver a powerful, compelling introduction that grabs attention and establishes your credibility. Your structure will help you include the right amount of information and the focus you desire. You'll learn how to make your content sticky and memorable.

## Chapter 5    Harness the Power of Stories

Learn to work with brain chemistry to use stories that hold your presentation together and make it both influential and memorable. Explore and learn to use three types of story structures.

## Chapter 6    Design Powerful Slide Decks

Avoid four common slide deck pitfalls and learn to use twelve power tips for deck design. Slides are only tools—they support you, not the other way around. Applying these design tips will save you time and ensure your deck is clear, concise and compelling.

## Chapter 7    Deliver Influentially

Prepare, practice and deliver with impact. Learn how to use positive body language and read your audience to adjust appropriately. Incorporate visualization, positive affirmations and other techniques to overcome anxiety.

Twenty-first century audiences have high expectations. They are giving you their very limited time and attention with the expectation that you will give them something valuable in return. The skills and tips in this book will help you design presentations with the right amount of information, with clear structure that captures the audience attention and leaves the audience feeling satisfied with the return on time investment in your presentation.

## Read this book AND PRACTICE to be a compelling presenter

As a result of reading this book, you will learn the skills to meet the expectations of your audiences and achieve your presentation objective every time. But reading a book will not change your presenting ability. To become a great presenter, you must apply these concepts and then practice, present and receive and incorporate feedback. It is my hope that you will become skilled at taking your audiences on presentation journeys. And perhaps you'll celebrate with a glass of wine after your next presentation.

Cheers!

## Resources

Lead 4 Success: Learn the Essentials of True Leadership by George Hallenbeck / Center for Creative Leadership

# CHAPTER 2

# Establish Your Objective

A compelling presentation takes the audience on a fascinating journey from where they are now to your ultimate destination—your presentation objective. To be successful, you need to be clear on the *why* of your presentation and bring the audience along to *know*, *feel* and *do* what you set out to accomplish.

*Michael, an accomplished scientist, worked for an innovative, market-leading life science organization. His assignment: to present to his company peers an update on the progress his division had made during the past six months. And they had made great progress—Michael was eager to talk about it.*

*He wanted to be sure everyone in his group felt represented, so he began the presentation by identifying each of the five group members and describing their backgrounds and specialty interests. He was delighted to be able to discuss their work, and it showed. He was very enthusiastic.*

*He introduced their current project with the history of the company's work in this area and a detailed recap of the milestones achieved. He moved on to discuss their plans for the work they were doing now and where they thought it would take them this year and next.*

*Michael tried not to get too technical, but he felt that people needed to have a certain amount of background in order to appreciate how hard his team had worked and how remarkable their accomplishments were.*

*The background information took about fifteen minutes to present. The present state of research took about ten minutes, and the plans for the next year took about fifteen minutes more.*

*When Michael finished, he fielded a couple of questions from the audience, and they politely clapped, but any observer could see that they had stopped listening long before Michael stopped speaking. What had happened to take this wonderfully intentioned opportunity down the road to audience forgetfulness?*

## If you don't have an objective, you can't achieve it

Michael's story is sadly a typical example of good intentions coupled with great knowledge failing to achieve much. Why? Because Michael lacked a clear, compelling presentation objective. *If you don't have an objective, you can't achieve it.*

Every well-constructed presentation starts by creating a clear, compelling objective. Michael's manager had simply told him to provide an update, and Michael felt he understood what that required: facts about where the project started, its current status and what could be expected in the future. Everything was focused on the science. But what was the update actually intended to achieve?

Michael had not thought through his objective—where did he want to take his audience? Why should they care? And what did he want them to know, feel and do as a result of the presentation? His fact-based approach wasn't directed toward a higher goal. And while everything he said was well researched and documented, he did not find a way to get the audience to see and feel what he wanted them to: *this work is important for the success of the company.*

Because having a clear, compelling objective is critical for an influential presentation, this book starts with helping you develop that objective.

## What's your destination?

Stephen Covey's bestselling book, *The Seven Habits of Highly Effective People*, includes this habit: begin with the end in mind. It applies perfectly to presentations.

Why is this presentation important to the audience, you, the organization or others? What do you want from your audience as a result of the presentation? Even a status update like Michael's should have a specific objective. You want to bring your audience along and influence them to know, feel or do what you set out to accomplish with your presentation.

Here are some examples of a presentation objective:

- Get approval to spend $25,000 for additional software licenses

- Convince lab partners to clean up the lab after each use

- Have Marketing agree to have new product literature ready one month before the product launches

Sometimes the *why* and *what* are not so obvious. Michael from the introductory example fell into an all-too-common trap when presenting 'updates' and 'overviews'—he pulled together lots of facts and figures, but he didn't really stop to think about why the audience should care or what he wanted to have happen as a result of the presentation.

Michael's *why* should have been to ensure ongoing commitment and support for this critical project. The audience should care about this project because they play a role, either directly or tangentially, in its success. And the success of the project leads to valuable customer solutions that contribute directly to much-needed, quantifiable organizational value.

Michael's *what* should have been for his audience to understand why and how they could support the project. He wanted the audience to feel appreciation for the amazing hard work the team had put in and would need to put in to reach the finish line. But he should have focused on what he wanted from the audience in terms of their continued support and commitment. To put a finer point on it, he should have had a specific vision of what that commitment would look like and directed his presentation toward that goal.

## Make sure your objective is clear

In addition to asking yourself *why* and *what*, you can strengthen your influence objective by addressing the following points:

- What is the problem you are addressing?

- What is your solution?

- What is the result that will be achieved with your solution?

To achieve your influential presentation objective, the objective must be clear and well-supported, as in the next example:

*A human resources leader is convinced that instituting a new work-from-home policy will make the company more competitive in recruiting and retaining top talent. It will also increase productivity, employee engagement and morale.*

**Presentation objective:** Get commitment to put a new work-from-home policy in place by the end of the next quarter to help retain and recruit top talent.

**Problem:** Currently, it takes too long to fill open positions (2.5 months), and our turnover rate is higher than industry average (28% vs. 18%). We've had 3 job offers to top talent rejected because we do not allow employees to work from home. In last quarter's exit interviews, 38% of departing employees mentioned not being able to work from home as a reason for leaving.

**Solution:** To adopt a work-from-home policy that will make us more competitive in the talent marketplace.

**Result:** We expect that this policy will improve our ability to attract and retain top talent. By making our employment brand more attractive, we believe that this policy will enable us to fill open positions in 6 weeks and cut our turnover by one-third.

For this presentation, here is the *know–feel–do*:

Know *about the problem*

Feel *frustrated with our current hiring and retention situation*

Do *support the approval and implementation of a new policy*

Note that although your objective should guide you as you create your presentation, you may or may not decide to share your objective explicitly with your audience. For some presentations, it may be appropriate to start with your objective:

*My objective today is to share pertinent new data that indicates we are losing current employees and are hindered in attracting top talent because we do not have a work-from-home policy.*

Starting with a story that captures audience attention and reveals your influence objective is another good opener:

*Josh was with the company for ten years and never expressed an interest in regularly working from home. Then his daughter was born, and like so many full-time employees with kids, Josh needed some additional work flexibility. He asked his manager if he could work from home two days a week. He committed to being available during our normal work hours and guaranteed that his work quantity and quality would not diminish. Due to his outstanding track record, Josh's manager petitioned Human Resources to grant the request. The answer was a resounding NO EXCEPTIONS. Josh now works from home for our competitor. Josh is not an isolated example. In reviewing exit interviews over the last year, 38% of those who left our company mentioned lack of a work-from-home policy as a reason for leaving. How many more can we afford to lose? And how many top job candidates will we lose because we don't have this flexibility? It's time for us to examine and adapt our policy so that we are competitive with 21st century work practices.*

No matter how you start—explicitly stating your objective or using a story to introduce the problem you're trying to solve—your objective must be front and center in the introduction of your presentation. As we'll talk about in more detail in later chapters, every slide should tie in to your presentation objective in some way—establishing it in the introduction, reinforcing it in the body and ensuring support for it in the conclusion.

Here are some other strategies to emphasize your influence objective throughout the presentation:

- *Challenge the audience to see why and how your objective is valuable*

- *Use examples that are familiar and memorable*
- *Use repetition to ensure the audience does not forget the objective*
- *Use simple graphics to depict and support your objective*
- Close the presentation not by summarizing, but by leading the audience to your desired conclusion

## Final checks

To help create an objective that will allow you to make a strong audience connection, ask yourself these questions:

*So what?* What content will be influential? Around what key ideas will I build my presentation?

*Who cares?* Will the people in the audience care about this presentation? If not, re-focus your objective so that the audience can appreciate why the objective is important to them.

*Why bother?* What difference will the information in this presentation make to your audience? Will going to the effort of creating and delivering this presentation influence future behavior?

Your objective also needs to be realistic in scope. Better to narrow the scope and accomplish your objective rather than trying to take on too much. An overly broad scope often leads to an over-stuffed, confusing presentation. If you can't state your objective concisely, consider paring it down.

Make sure that the objective is appropriate for the audience. We'll discuss tailoring your presentation to your audience in more detail in the next chapter, but it's crucial that the people you will be presenting to are actually in a position to support your objective. Similar to adjusting your scope, you may need to tweak your original objective to match the roles and knowledge base reflected in the audience.

And of course, ensure that your objective can be accomplished in the amount of time that is available for your presentation. Rushing through your slides or going over your allotted time—losing your audience 'in the moment'—will undo all the groundwork you've laid in preparation.

## Summary of Key Ideas

- Think of your presentation as a journey. You must know your destination before you start. Your presentation objective is your destination.

- Your presentation objective includes the *why* and the *what* of your presentation:

  *Why* this is important to the audience, you, the organization, others?

  *Why* should the audience care?

  *What* do you want the audience to know, feel and do?

- To ensure your objective is clear, ask yourself these questions:

  *What* is the problem you are addressing?

  *What* is your solution?

  *What* is the result that will be achieved with your solution?

## Put This to Work

1. What is the *why* of your presentation? Why is it important to this audience? Why should the audience care?

2. What do you want people to *know, feel* and *do*?

3. Clarify your objective:

    a. What is the problem you are addressing?

    b. What is your solution?

    c. What is the result that will be achieved with your solution?

4. Considering your responses to the items above, write out your presentation objective.

5. How will you know if this presentation is successful?

6. What feedback would you like to see about this presentation after the audience has time to evaluate it?

## Resources

Stephen Covey, *The Seven Habits of Highly Effective People*, 1989.

# CHAPTER 3

# Make a Strong Audience Connection

Let's assume you have a clear objective for your presentation. Great! You know where you want to go—but what about your audience? Too often, we see presenters bolt off on the journey without noticing that they've lost their passengers along the way. To be influential, you need to compel your audience to come with you by cutting concisely to the information they need.

*Jessica, a very successful product manager, knew her product line incredibly well. She visited customers who used the products, routinely talked to the research staff who created them, and was enthusiastic about them. Sometimes, overly enthusiastic.*

*Jessica's manager asked her to present the latest and greatest about her products to the sales force at the annual sales meeting. She was more than happy to accept. She had introduced two new products at last year's meeting, and they were exceeding expectations in the market. She couldn't wait to tell everyone what was coming this year.*

*Jessica's objective was to provide the sales team with what they needed to know in order to exceed* their sales quotas for her product line in the next 12 months. She intended to cover the following items in her presentation: (1) share product development background and finished product specifications; (2) demonstrate how her products are superior to competitors' products; and (3) describe the value proposition.

Her introduction was full of market statistics, with last year's targets and results. Her slides contained incredible amounts of detail about product trials and outcomes proving the competitive superiority of the new products. She jumped into this year's targets and why the new products were going to outperform the competition. She went into great detail about the market research that went into creating the value proposition.

But looking around the room, it was obvious that the audience was not picking up her enthusiasm. Ten minutes into her thorough, detailed presentation, the glazed expressions on the faces in the audience made it clear that many had checked out. As this registered with Jessica, her reaction was to talk faster and more emphatically.

She finished her presentation by making bold claims about how successful the sales people would be, how they would be winning sales awards and bonuses with the new product line. She received the usual polite clapping that usually means the audience appreciates your leaving the stage. What went wrong?

## Invest the Time to Know Your Audience

Jessica created the presentation solely from her own point of view. She knew where she wanted to take the audience on the journey, yet she didn't make the right kind of connections with the audience so that they would join her. She included plenty of detailed information about *what* the new products were, but she failed to get to the specifics on *how* the sales reps could use this information successfully in the field. How could she have done better?

Jessica needed to start by understanding who she was presenting to. Had she focused on their need (to know how to successfully sell the product), rather than her own (to reach cumulative sales targets), she most likely would have had the full attention of the audience throughout the journey.

Taking the time to assess your audience puts you in the best position to connect with them, which in turn puts you in the best position to influence them. You will not be compelling unless you have a clear understanding of the emotional and organizational needs of your audience. Whether you are presenting to colleagues who know you well or a room full of strangers, you can strengthen your presentation by tailoring your approach to each audience. This chapter outlines the key questions you should try to answer about your audience before you begin creating your presentation:

- Who is attending?

- What do they already know about your topic?

- What do they need to know—to meet their own aims and to meet your influence objective?

- How do they make decisions?

Then we discuss how you can leverage that knowledge to influence.

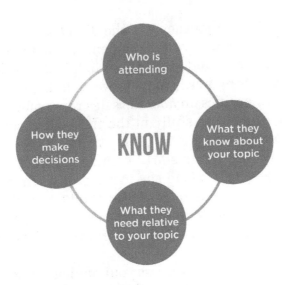

## Who is attending?

Making a strong audience connection starts with understanding who will be in the seats. When you agree to make a presentation, be sure you spend the time necessary to get answers to some basic questions about your audience. Your presentation sponsor is usually the best person to help you learn about who will be in attendance.

The following types of audience insights may not always be available to you. However, when you can get this information, you are in a position to fine-tune your presentation even further to increase your influence.

### Organizational position

What positions do your attendees hold? What is their level of decision-making authority? What is their sphere of influence? Budget authority?

It is important to target your appeal to the right level. Understand who has decision-making authority, controls budgets, etc. Seek to understand what roles the members of the audience can play in helping you to achieve your objective given their position in the company.

## Demographics

Find out as much as you can about demographics. Start with the basics: age range/generation (Baby Boomers, Millennials, Gen Y), education, gender.

Knowing this will help you anticipate how to adapt your communication style and present at a knowledge level that is appropriate for your audience.

## Psychographics

Psychographics is the study and classification of people based on their values, attitudes, interests and aspirations. Knowing audience psychographics enables you to frame your presentation to connect with values, attitudes and interests. You can structure your content and adapt your delivery to be on the same wavelength.

## Ethnographics

What cultural and social insights can you glean?

We live in a global economy. You can demonstrate your professionalism by being respectful of different social and cultural influences in your audience. Knowing these differences will enable you to adapt examples and stories to ensure positive connections and avoid unintentional gaffes.

## Firmographics

Gather insights into the types of industries, companies, business focus, organization size (revenues and/or employees), global footprint, competitive position, etc. that will be represented in the audience.

When presenting to individuals outside of your organization, knowing firmographic information allows you to tailor your message, incorporate appropriate examples and make references that are on target geographically.

# What does the audience already know, and what do they need to know?

It is essential to create content that resonates with your audience, adding to their existing knowledge without duplicating it. Few people want to devote their precious time to hearing about what they already know. Assessing what your audience knows enables you to present the right information at the right level of detail to capture and retain attention.

Equally important, is what your audience knows accurate? Current? Provide accurate, irrefutable evidence to help your audience see the situation in the same frame you see it.

Most people agree to attend a presentation because they want something: information, ideas, answers, direction, etc. Ask yourself the following questions about your audiences' needs and expectations:

## Why is this audience giving you their time?

Imagine yourself in your audience and ask the question they will be asking: *What's in it for me?* As you create content, be sure you are including information that will be most important for this audience. That information should be clear, both in terms of *how* it is presented and in *why* it is important, in order for the audience to think it's worth their time and attention.

Finding out what the audience needs can be accomplished in a variety of ways. Reaching out directly to several individuals who will be attending your presentation is the best, most direct way to gain insights. If that is not possible, ask the individual who is sponsoring your presentation to give you ideas on what would benefit the audience the most. If you can get a list of attendees' names, spend some time checking out their LinkedIn profiles. Look for experience, education and interests. You can use this information to establish connections.

Let's go back to Jessica. A conversation with a few sales reps or a sales manager about what the sales force needs to sell new products would have helped her create content that captured audience attention. They needed practical, specific information about these products, like how they compare to the competition, how to price in different target markets and how to use the sales tools and samples that were available.

## What are their problems, concerns and challenges relative to your topic?

To capture attention and hold it, focus on the things that cause problems for your audience. People are highly motivated to pay attention when they believe you can help them find a solution to a pressing problem.

In fact, research indicates that executive-level decision-makers are 70 percent more willing to make a decision to change if you position their current situation in terms of what they stand to lose by not changing versus what they could gain by changing[1]. We are more likely to make a decision to avoid pain or loss than to gain benefits.

Identify the professional challenges your audience shares and start your presentation by focusing there. Your audience will see that you relate to their real world. And they'll want to stay tuned to find out what information you have to help solve this challenge.

## How receptive will they be to your content?

If you are presenting information that challenges the status quo, expect your audience to be uncomfortable and perhaps even skeptical. You will need to build a strong case that connects with both the left brain and the right brain to be successful in changing opinions and behavior. Challenging a person's beliefs can stir emotions ranging from curiosity to skepticism to defensiveness. Audience members may be curious about the new claims but may also be skeptical and want to defend current beliefs.

To influence when challenging the status quo, you will need to use logic and provide evidence. Gain agreement on what the overarching problem is for which you are presenting a solution that is different. Be specific about a problem that is real, pressing and familiar. Next, identify the current generally accepted best solution. Then compare your alternative to the current solution. Identify factually and logically both how and why your solution is better. Provide evidence: case studies, testimonials. Last, focus on what your solution will mean to the audience on a personal level and try to see your content from their perspective. Point out how your solution will save time, increase returns, enhance credibility, etc.

## How does your topic impact basic needs?

In addition to the specifics outlined above, consider how your influence objective can touch upon some of the universal human needs that your audience is likely to be sensitive to. Tapping into specific perceived needs like the ones shown in the next illustration is likely to trigger emotional responses that can have a huge influence on decision-making. We'll talk more about harnessing the power of these emotions in the later section on leveraging audience knowledge to influence.

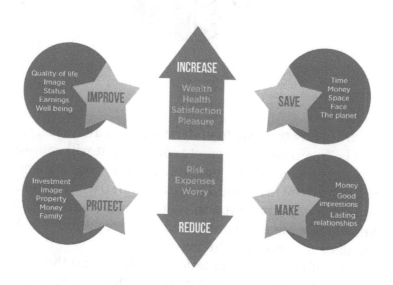

## How does the audience make decisions?

People tend to make decisions using emotions, and then justify those decisions using logic. Therefore, to successfully influence, you must appeal to both the emotional side of the brain—using stories, examples and feelings—and to the logical side of the brain, which relies on facts, data and reason.

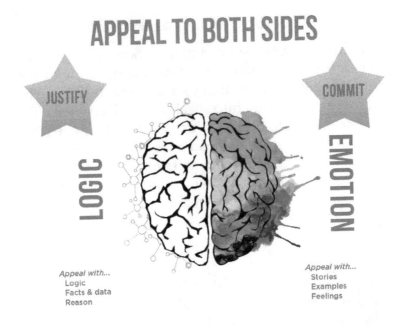

By taking the time to understand your audience, you will be in a position to create content that will connect both emotionally and logically. Relating to your audience will contribute to a critical success factor: trust. This adds to your credibility, as you will come across as thoughtful, knowledgeable and competent. And credibility opens the door to positive influence.

An influential presentation is able to find the right blend of these two ingredients—emotion and logic—to maximize its impact, and what works best for one audience may not work at all for another. This is where your previous background research comes in: given what you know about the audience's knowledge base, major motivations and worries, trends in their industry, etc., *how does all this impact the way they make decisions?*

## Decision-making styles

Susan Finerty's book, *The Cross-Functional Influence Playbook,* identifies the characteristics of four unique types of decision makers. Here are some ideas on how to influence each one:

| Decision-Making Style | Influence Strategy |
|---|---|
| **INNOVATOR** Likes new ideas. Focus is on problem-solving. Thinks about the big picture and the bottom line. Results are important. Likes to inspire and be inspired. | Make the case for how your solution provides specific results. Demonstrate how solution fits into big picture. Describe how solution is new, different. Provide examples that inspire. |
| **IMITATOR** Prefers following successful examples. Dislikes risk and conflict. Deliberate when taking action and making decisions. | Provide successful examples and testimonials. Explain how risk is reduced with your solution. Use guarantees if possible. |
| **ANALYTIC** Logical and risk-averse. Relies heavily on data and analysis. Details are important. Prefers solid structure and organization. | Get into the details: be prepared with the specifics of your solution. Provide solid, tangible, practical evidence. Use appropriate jargon. |
| **HANDS-ON** Likes to have their ideas center stage. If not their idea, then wants to play a role in shaping the outcome. Likes to be involved and control the outcome. | If possible, pre-sell your idea. Get input and include it in your presentation. Give credit. Demonstrate how this person can play a leading role, if appropriate. |

Consider this chart in parallel with the graphic on page 33.

*Innovators are typically seeking to increase, make and improve.*

*Imitators usually want to reduce, protect and save.*

*Analytics want to protect, save and improve.*

*Hands-on are drawn to improve, protect and make.*

Each audience is unique, and most will have a combination of the various types of decision-makers.

If your presentation objective is to gain agreement for a specific request, you will no doubt know who the ultimate decision-makers in the room are. Be sure to structure your content and frame the decision in a way that addresses the needs and decision-making styles of those individuals.

If your presentation objective is to change the opinion of the audience, determine the likely decision-making style for the majority of the audience. For instance, an audience made up primarily of scientists most likely will be analytics. Therefore, include facts, figures and details around a problem and the specific solution you are proposing. Show how to minimize risk. Provide proof and testimonials.

An audience made up primarily of C-suite leaders will most likely be innovators. They need to be inspired and prefer to focus on the big picture and how new solutions fit into achieving results. Start at a high level that focuses on how your solution is new, different and how it will lead to success.

Imagine you are the project lead for a technology team that has just received a patent for a revolutionary new technology. This technology has the ability to transform how data is encrypted, making it virtually impossible to be hacked. Your company intends to license the use of this technology to a handful of companies in a variety of different industries. You have two upcoming presentation opportunities to explain what this technology is and how it will change the world. Here's you how you might adapt your presentation for each audience:

|  | AUDIENCE A Technical product managers and product development engineers. These individuals are expected to bring next-generation products to the market. They are mostly Millennials and mostly male. | AUDIENCE B Non-technical, business-development specialists looking for new product and market opportunities, mostly Gen X, equal mix male/female. |
| --- | --- | --- |
| Presentation objective | Convince the audience of the technology's • superiority vs. status quo • safety • ease of incorporating into products | Convince the audience that this technology will • extend product life cycles • open up significant new markets • be a wise investment • provide a competitive advantage |
| Create your presentation objective to | Focus on how the technology will provide them with the opportunity to change the world, make a positive difference, increase collaboration and enhance diversity by enabling safe global access to data. Geek focus: get into the technology | Focus on what the technology will do to shape markets, how it will make work less risky, how quickly and easily it will provide a return on investment. Technology as hero. Appeal to forward thinking. Layman focus: don't wade too deep into the Technology |

# Leverage your knowledge to influence strategically: the 6 influence levers

You've done your audience homework. You know who will be attending, what they know about your topic, what they need, why they're attending and how they decide. Now it's time to choose your influence approach to ensure you make a strong audience connection.

Over the years we've experienced and employed many of the well-researched principles of influence and persuasion. While there are many models and levers, most influence revolves around six basic approaches. Here are the approaches and how to employ them in influential business presentations.

## Reason & logic

*What*
Reason is the capacity for consciously making sense of things, establishing and verifying facts, and changing or justifying practices, institutions, and beliefs based on new or existing information. Logic means providing a formal, scientific way of assessing things. This approach won't always secure buy-in, but without it, many people will not give your ideas a chance.

*How*
Provide verifiable facts and figures. Build your case. Provide testimonials, examples and proof.

*When to use*
Almost always when your audience expects you to present the facts and rationale that support your conclusions—the objectives of your presentation. When the audience is made up of fact seekers and experienced, knowledgeable

people who will emotionally reject conclusions presented without compelling evidence, you will need to use several aspects of reasoning, from raw data, to collection methodology to statistical analysis to break through the emotional barriers they have set up, which are their preconditions to finding you credible enough to believe.

## Give to get

*What*: When you give, you have a higher probability of getting something in return. This is the psychological principle of reciprocity: If I get something of value from you, I feel more inclined to give you something.

*How*: Give information, ideas, support, your time, inspiration, content, something that helps the audience. Be specific about what you hope to get in return.

> *Today I am going to give you access to tools that will save you 20 minutes a day. In return, I am going to ask you to commit to using these tools for one week.*

*When to use*: Use this approach when the audience has no preconditions for accepting your conclusions and call to action. They have no negative emotional barriers; your presentation should support the potential positives of doing something in return for a benefit that you can capably describe in terms that are attractive to them. This is often useful when there is no provably "right" answer, and there are several alternatives available. With your personality and arguments, you may be able to show the audience it is in their interest to give whatever you're suggesting a reasonable try. You need to show the reasonability of what you are asking, show the practicality of doing it and be clear about the potential benefits.

## Urgency

*What*: The psychological principle of urgency causes people to suspend deliberate thought and act quickly.

*How*: A sense of urgency can be created through scarcity: time running out, or greater demand than supply. Demonstrating that your solution can help people avoid pain or loss also creates a sense of urgency.

> *We did not adequately anticipate the incredible demand for this new product. If we do not produce 30% more per month over the next three months, we risk losing market share to our competitors.*

*When to use*: You need to prove strong cause-and-effect relationships that appeal to reason and logic as well as understand the emotional underpinnings of this audience. They need to believe that your claims of urgency are credible and that they have something to lose by not acting on them. You need to have some understanding of the experience/knowledge background of the audience, their biases, their potential fears, and be sure you are not proposing something they've seen and rejected several times previously.

## Authority / Power

*What*: Authority can be derived from having a position of power in an organization with the right to give orders, make decisions and enforce obedience. Authority can also derive from having deep knowledge and expertise.

*How*: When appropriate, rely on your position or title by demonstrating that you have experience and have earned the title and deserve respect. If you are an authority with deep knowledge and expertise, provide examples and stories that help the audience understand why you are credible and authoritative.

> *This situation is very similar to the Shaughnessy impact that occurred in our industry 15 years ago. At that time, we acted quickly and decisively to draft industry guidelines that are still in effect today to protect our customers. We must lead the way again in this instance.*

*When to use*: It is easier to say when not to try this influence level: when you don't have any credible, recognizable authority or power. Claiming to have relationships that seem even slightly unlikely (I worked with Richard Feynman or studied under Christiaan Barnard) raises the suspicion of audiences that you are not authentic. They then focus their energy on exploring that claimed relationship and pay no attention to what you hope to get them to do. This is definitely an influence avenue you should test on peers to see if it comes across positively before you use it on an audience. However, if you can credibly make such claims, you instantly cross over any emotional barriers to acceptance of your claims or your efforts to move the audience.

## Aspiration

*What*: Aspiration is the hope or ambition of achieving, owning and/or becoming. People aspire to such things because of personal motivators.

*How*: Identify what your audience might aspire to. Aspirations can include emulating someone (like an accomplished professional or athlete), achieving a greater good (to promote environmental sustainability, reduce poverty, etc.) or making a difference in a significant way (reduce cancer, provide clean water in developing countries, encourage acceptance of others, etc.).Very personal aspirations may also apply, such as making money, losing weight or living a long and healthy life.

> *Few individuals have the talent and ability to achieve greatness like athletic heroes such as Michael Jordan, Mia Hamm or Michael Phelps. But you can be a great hero in an important way. You can be a mentor and make a positive difference in others' lives.*

*When to use*: If you have great familiarity with the audience and understand the nature of their positive aspirations, this is a wonderful influence factor to work into your presentation. Shared aspirations can lead to trust. Their emotional barriers to accepting your recommendations will be lowered significantly by your efforts to show that taking the actions you suggest will promote their own aspirations. You become one of them; not an outsider whom they must guard themselves against.

## Likability

*What*: "People buy from people they like." We tend to like people who are more similar to us. But likability, being easily liked, is possible even when presenting to very dissimilar audiences.

*How*: Smile! Greet people by name. Use open, confident, positive body language, as discussed in detail in chapter 8. Know your audience to connect with them on their terms, their interests. Help your audience see that you understand their challenges. Be sincere, real and vulnerable. Reveal why you are passionate about your topic.

*When to use*: When you have had enough exposure to people in the audience to realize you like them, like what they are doing, and admire their efforts and accomplishments, you will be able to genuinely reflect those feelings to them. They will read your liking of them, and it will impact their emotional reaction to you. Typically, that will lead to your being found likeable. However, this is not an influence factor to try to force, that is, to try to create likability when there is nothing behind it. An appearance of false or forced behavior will set up emotional barriers that are very difficult to overcome.

## Final audience connection comments

Assess each presentation to determine which influence factor or factors will work best for your audience. Remember: even the same presentation content may benefit from different influence factors depending on who is in the audience.

Let's go back to Jessica from the introductory example. The specific influence levers that might have worked in her situation include

> **Give to Get**: *I am here to give you all of the information you need to successfully sell my products so that you will achieve your sales quota.*

> **Likability**: *I'm on your side! We share the same goal of solving customers' problems. You can trust me*

*because I need you to succeed so I will succeed. I'm the expert on the product and the market, and I am here to help you succeed with my knowledge and expertise.*

Influence starts with understanding your audience so you can capture and hold their attention throughout your journey. The following chapters will delve into the skills you need to successfully navigate that journey to your influence objective in every business presentation.

## Summary of Key Ideas

- Understanding your audience helps you to make a positive, memorable connection

- Do your homework to know

  - Who is attending

  - What they know about your topic

  - What they need relative to your topic

  - How they make decisions

- With audience insights, you can adapt your content, stories, examples and delivery to get on the same wavelength and build your credibility

- There are 6 universal influence levers that you can incorporate into your presentation to increase your impact on an audience

    Reason and logic

    Give to get

    Urgency

    Authority/power

    Aspiration

    Likability

## Put This to Work

1. Who is in your audience?
   Describe your audience. Include what you know with respect to individuals' positions/roles, demographics, psychographics, ethnographics, firmographics.
2. What does the audience know about your topic? What does this audience expect to gain in return for the time invested with you?
3. What does the audience need relative to your topic?
   - Why is this audience giving you their time? What do they expect to get in return?
   - What are the audience problems, concerns and challenges relative to your topic?
   - What perspectives might the audience have that differ from yours? How receptive will they be to your content?
   - What are the basic needs relative to your topic?
   - What does the audience want to improve / increase / save / protect / reduce / make?
   - Why will the audience trust me?
4. How do the key decision makers make decisions?
5. Which of the six influence levers will work best for your audience?

## Resources

[1] State of the Conversation Report "Decide or Defer: What Message Gets Executive Decision-Makers to Buy Now Instead of Never?" https://win.corporatevisions.com/rs/413-YED-439/images/Report-Decide-or-Defer.pdf

Susan Z. Finerty, *The Cross-Functional Influence Playbook*, 2016

# CHAPTER 4

# Create Compelling Content

As you begin to develop the content of your presentation, you need to continue to work with an audience-centered mindset. If you give the audience something of value, you will get their attention. You want them to grasp the reasoning behind your approach quickly while having it stick with them because it resonates or creates an emotional reaction. This combination of logic and emotion will influence the audience to respond positively to your point of view or call to action.

*Even at an international company chock full of talent, Ed stood out as an up-and-comer in corporate finance who had the ear of most of the C-suite. It didn't seem to matter whether the subject was valuing an acquisition, transfer pricing or deferred taxes—Ed was out in front consulting and advising.*

*The CFO had been having Ed prepare his presentations to the Executive Committee and Board of Directors. By investing time in understanding the individual views and business frames of these leaders, Ed tailored presentations to deliver information that, as a group, everyone wanted, and that Ed knew they needed in order to make decisions.*

Despite his nearly encyclopedic knowledge of the business and particularly the financial aspects of it, Ed did not use facts and statistics as his primary tools in these presentations. Ed built his entire approach around finishing strongly. He created each main point around a business issue that he could frame in two or three ways. He would run the framing process by the CFO to determine the best strategies to accomplish the purpose and objectives of the presentation. And when he drew conclusions, he tested them with several people beforehand to understand what kind of reactions he could expect. That helped him frame those conclusions to generate the finish he desired.

He did not try to show support using several numeric approaches. He had alternative approaches in the background to use in case of challenging questions, but his claim to fame was that he made finance appear simple.

Because he explored audience concerns in advance, Ed generally picked a great starting point that held the attention of these high-powered audiences. By not overwhelming them with facts, charts and extended analyses, he could focus his energy on ensuring that they knew where the presentation was going and why. It always seemed that the questions asked were ones Ed was very well prepared to answer. He never tried to BS anyone, and if someone wanted more facts, Ed would somehow manage to give them a memo that very day on the subject. He understood how these time-pressured people wanted to get their information both during and after a presentation, and he made it his business to give them what they wanted.

Ed exemplifies the power of presentations as a key aspect of business that combines acumen, networking and great structure. He eventually became CFO and

*Chairman of the Board of one of the largest companies in the world.*

## Structure for clarity and memorability

To increase the probability of influencing your audience and accomplishing your objective, start with a solid structure. Remembering our metaphor of the presentation as a journey, the structure of your presentation is akin to a trip itinerary. You must know where you want to take the audience along the way.

What does great structure look like? It is really this straightforward, but don't mistake this for easy:

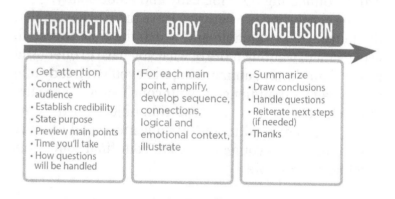

## Structure in three parts

Your introduction plays a critical role: you need to interest the audience and get them to go on this journey with you. You absolutely must start with an introduction that grabs attention. People are so overwhelmed by the complexity of work, relationships, their own needs and wants, that they have great difficulty paying much attention to anything else. Your job is to break mental preoccupation so the audience can focus on you and your presentation.

The introduction is where you lay out the itinerary for your journey. You must capture attention, connect with your audience and establish your credibility. Whew! That's a lot to get done in a short amount of time. This is also where you want to let your audience know where you are taking them on this journey: state your purpose and preview your main points. Finally, the introduction is where you need to manage expectations. How long will you be presenting, and how do you want to handle questions?

In the body of your presentation, you lead them where you want to go. Present each main point and provide proof, connecting both logically and emotionally.

The conclusion is where you leave them believing that the journey was valuable and worth the time invested, leaving them wanting more of what you have to offer. And rather than simply summarizing what you've already told them, lead your audience to your conclusion. Make sure that you achieve your presentation objective. In some cases, you may need to address questions and identify next steps during your conclusion. Your final comments must be memorable.

The two most important parts of your presentation are the ones most people spend the least amount of time preparing: the conclusion and introduction. Your audience will most likely remember what you say last: this is the recency principle. So, start your presentation by working on your conclusion. How will you drive your presentation objective home in your conclusion? As we discussed in chapter two, you need to begin with the end in mind. Have the end of the journey plugged into your GPS.

The second most important part of your presentation is the introduction. If you don't begin strong and capture attention, then the work you did on preparing the rest of the presentation may not matter. Work on your introduction second. How will you capture attention? How will you establish your credibility?

After you write your conclusion and your introduction, it will be much easier to create the body content. Remember that less is more. Fewer main points are easier to remember. Resist the temptation to over-stuff your presentation. Structure using main points and subpoints. Amplify each point using the subpoints. Provide proof and examples.

Let's explore each of these sections a bit more.

## Conclusion: Finish strong

The conclusion is where you ensure you accomplish your presentation objective. This 3- to 5-minute space is your final opportunity to be compelling. Here are a few things you can do to finish strong:

### Have a clear, powerful conclusion, not just an ending

Summarizing your presentation isn't the same as having a conclusion. A powerful conclusion brings closure to your topic and ensures that you accomplish your presentation objective. The best conclusions are also short and memorable. If you have a specific call to action, this is the place for it.

## Tie back to your introduction

If you used a story in your introduction, tie your final comments back to that story. Finish the story here and make the specific connection as to how that relates to your objective.

Just like world class gymnasts, you need to focus on nailing the landing!

## Be creative, compelling and energetic

Remember, humans are emotional and make decisions with emotions. Don't be afraid to demonstrate or discuss how your topic has touched you or others emotionally. You will set yourself apart and be memorable by being creative in your conclusion. Keep your energy high all the way to the end.

It is not necessary to summarize your main points in every presentation. The old presentation adage of "tell 'em what you told 'em" may actually diminish the power of your conclusion.

If you answer questions after your concluding remarks, be sure to repeat your conclusion in one sentence as you close your presentation. You want the audience to leave with the most important message in their minds.

## Conclusion example

At the end of a quarterly results presentation, the speaker chose to briefly summarize the main points and then conclude with a rallying approach:

> *These results indicate that we have a lot to be proud of. Revenue is above plan. Profitability is on target.*

*We're keeping costs in check. The key to continuing this performance is supporting all customer-facing organizations. I encourage each of you to spend time each week learning about their challenges and doing all you can to remove any roadblocks to success. Let's ensure that we are the ones that make it possible for our teams to exceed all plan targets.*

## Introduction: start strong

Remember that your introduction has a lot to accomplish. The most important initial question the audience asks about a presentation is *"Why should I care?"* Capturing the attention of your audience is easy—*if* you put the effort into making a strong connection. But you have very little time to get the audience on your side.

The hook that engages your audience in the introduction must be incredibly concise. Research shows that your opening comments and presence receive about 15 to 20 seconds of uninterrupted audience attention. If your speaking rate is about 150 words per minute, that means your first 35 to 50 words have to be perfectly crafted. Here are several ways to start strong:

### Focus on a problem

Instead of tantalizing your audience with benefits, start by focusing on a compelling problem. Be graphic. Provide examples. Draw the audience into the problem emotionally and perhaps even make them a bit uncomfortable. Humans are more motivated to avoid pain and loss than to pursue pleasure and gain. This is known as loss aversion. So, begin your presentation by stimulating your audience to avoid a problem. Your goal is to influence them to move in the direction of accepting your solution, and so you achieve your presentation objective.

Our efforts to address our supply chain issues over the last three months have not produced the results we hoped for. Our primary packaging supplier missed two critical deadlines. The integration of our new software was 5 weeks late. And the move to our new warehouse in Charlotte caused our fulfillment to drop by 14%. In spite of our efforts, the light at the end of the tunnel seems more like an oncoming train.

## Use a benefit statement

If you've done your homework and you know the needs of your audience, you can open in a very targeted way. A benefit statement essentially tells the audience why it is important to pay attention: they are going to get something specific and useful from their time invested with you.

> *In the next 30 minutes I will show you how to gain control over your time and your lab budget by reducing test time by 25% and increasing test yield by 40%.*

## Challenge the status quo

Be provocative. Start by challenging what the audience believes to be true. They may become annoyed, even defensive, and will want to stay tuned to see how you are going to prove your challenge.

> *Your overall health may depend less on exercise and more on what you eat. Seventy percent of your overall health is determined by the health of your gut. It may*

*be more valuable for you to spend time learning how to eat right rather than to exercise.*

## Audience participation

You need to be careful with this one. The typical rhetorical question does not count as audience participation. In fact, many people are annoyed with rhetorical questions, as they can be deemed silly or even unprofessional. For example: *Who likes discovering that their voice mailbox is full?* (As you raise your hand to indicate how the audience should respond.)

Asking a question to gauge audience understanding or impact does qualify as audience participation: *Raise your hand when I mention the percentage of time you spend dealing with email on an average day.* This provides an opportunity for the audience to weigh in and see where their experience is relative to others in the room.

## Personal observation

This makes it personal and helps establish your credibility: *In the last five years, I've conducted research that proves theory XYZ is wrong.* What? You can prove this? Show me. This opening sets you up to provide the proof in the body of your presentation.

## Tell a compelling story

The topic of storytelling is hot right now. Why? Because society is coming to appreciate the power of stories on a new level. Storytelling is as old as humankind. We tell stories to make sense of life, to share what we know and to connect with others. Well-crafted stories are memorable, engaging and instructive, all at once. They can change the way the audience feels (excited, enraged, motivated, etc.), and as such, they have a unique power to influence—so much so that the whole next chapter is about how to use stories to their full potential. Suffice to say here that a story can be a great way to grab your audience's attention at the start of your presentation.

If you use a personal story, your goal is to get the audience to feel the way you feel. A few Octobers ago (think pink ribbons everywhere), I was asked to give a talk at a breast cancer fundraising event. I wanted to change the focus of discussion from cancer *awareness* to cancer *prevention* and encourage the audience to consider four cancer prevention techniques. To get their attention, I started with this:

> *I hate cancer. I hate what it does to those going through cancer and to those who love them. Three years ago, I spent a blustery April evening in a Columbus, Ohio, restaurant with Donna, a friend I've known for more than half my life. This high-energy mother of three had just completed her second round of radiation and chemotherapy in her battle against raging breast cancer. In fact, this was her second go-around with cancer, having survived thyroid cancer 12 years before.*
>
> *Fatigue was her nemesis. It was so sad to see her energy level dwindle as we ate our way through the evening, from the antipasto salad (high energy) to the veggie pizza (moderate energy) to the lemon sorbet (running on empty). It was like watching the air go out of a balloon.*
>
> *When we got back to her house, she explained her evening routine. Much like Cinderella's transformation at the stroke of midnight, Donna turned into Mrs. Potato Head before bed. Mrs. Potato Head? Off came the wig, exposing a perfectly shaped bald pate. Out*

came the contacts, replaced with glasses. Off with the makeup, revealing a sickly, pale complexion. And finally, off went the mastectomy bra, leaving no doubt that her once attractive figure was now only possible with assistance from Maidenform. She truly was Mrs. Potato Head as her parts and accessories came off.

Cancer is vicious. It not only robs people of their health, but also of dignity. Donna was able to laugh about her Mrs. Potato Head transformation with me because that allowed her to deal with her situation. She still cried when she was alone.

We spend a lot of time every October talking about early detection of breast cancer. I believe we need to spend more time talking about prevention of breast cancer. You can fight back. You can take action to prevent breast cancer. Groundbreaking research from the University of California, San Diego, has shown that vitamin D3 has the potential to reduce breast cancer by 67%. Stay tuned as I share this and three additional techniques to help prevent breast cancer from turning you and those you love into Mrs. Potato Head.

This two-and-a-half-minute personal story is designed to bring everyone's natural fear of breast cancer to the surface, so they feel it in the moment strongly enough to take action to prevent it.

Stories from your own life come alive when you tell them. They are your own mini-reality show, with your own, real emotions. *That* engages your audience.

## Body: leading the audience through your journey of proof

The body is where you lay out your case that influences the audience to accept your presentation objective. It is critical to be concise here as well. First, identify your main points. Remember: less is more. Most of us can remember three main points. More than three is hard for many of us to recall.

For each main point, what are your subpoints? What proof can you provide for each of these? Statistics, graphs and examples provide credibility and appeal to the logical side of our brains. But don't forget to add detailed, specific descriptions that will appeal to the emotional side as well.

### How not to begin

As important as knowing how to begin is knowing how NOT to begin. Here are some of the openings we've seen that are guaranteed to blow your opportunity to capture attention and establish your credibility:

X *Start by thanking the audience*

This puts you in a one-down position and suggests that your time is less important than theirs.

X *Start by saying "Before I begin..."*

How annoying. Just begin!

X *Start with a cartoon*

Rather lame. While a cartoon may break preoccupation, you risk creating a diversion and distracting your audience, taking them off topic.

X *Open with a quote*

Start with your own words, not someone else's.

### Start with an outline

Rather than open up a blank presentation template to start creating, we suggest you build your presentation by outlining it first. The options that we find work best for outlining include using index cards, Post-it® notes or—if you need to work electronically—a blank deck of plain white slides.

Using this approach allows you to easily see how much content you have and to quickly try different ordering. If using cards or Post-its, you can easily move things around. Or, if using software to lay out your presentation, it should give you the option to see all your slides from a bird's eye view (in PowerPoint, this is the Slide Sorter view). Use this setting to assess the flow and organization.

Start with one card/Post-it/slide for your conclusion: write the bullet point for your conclusion. Be sure this focuses the audience on your objective: the *why* of your presentation.

Next, do the same for your introduction: write the bullet point for your introduction. Again, focus on the *why* of your presentation.

For the body, use one card/Post-it/slide for each of your main points.

Now that you have the main components of your presentation, add additional cards to fill in the content, details, etc.

Does the order flow? If not, change it up. This approach helps you to sort, sift and organize content logically. It will also help you avoid over-stuffing your presentation. This approach will also help save time, preventing you from developing content you later discard.

*Key point:* To increase audience retention of your content, strive to make the presentation structure as simple as possible.

## Make your content sticky

Now that you have your structure in place, you can flesh out the content to make it memorable or "sticky." Here are some strategies for stickiness.

### Use the Problem–Solution–Result format

The Problem–Solution–Result format draws attention to a specific problem that the audience cares about. Present your overarching problem in the introduction. Then break the problem down to its main points and sub-points in the body, providing your solution for each main point. You can also share the *which means that* result for each main point as you go.

*Problem:* Lab testing for XYZ takes too long
*Solution:* Automate steps 4 through 6
*Result:* Which means that you will save 30 minutes per test and will have more time to spend on analysis

### Repetition

Another technique for increasing stickiness is to use repetition. Repeating your central message several times in the right places increases the likelihood of the message sticking mentally. Simon Sinek does this successfully by repeating the phrase, "People don't buy what you do, they buy why you do it" five times throughout his 18-minute TED talk, "How Great Leaders Inspire Action." Dr. Martin Luther King repeated "I have a dream" eight times throughout his famous speech on the Washington Mall in 1963.

## The Rule of Three

Humans are adept at remembering things that come in threes:

*Life, liberty and the pursuit of happiness*
*The good, the bad and the ugly*
*Reduce, reuse, recycle*
*Speak no evil, see no evil, hear no evil*
*Stop, drop and roll*
*There are three kinds of lies: lies, damned lies and statistics*

## Similarity

Like attracts like. Make a comparison that shows how your point is like something else that is very familiar to your audience. The process for this is very much like changing a tire on your car. Remove the lug nuts, take off the tire, replace with a new tire and replace the lug nuts.

## Novelty and surprise

Create fascination with things that are different, unique, unfamiliar. For example, in 2009, Bill Gates gave a TED talk on mosquitoes and malaria prevention. To help the audience connect to his topic, he used a somewhat shocking approach: "Malaria is of course transmitted by mosquitoes," he announced to the crowd before opening a jar of the insects (which were not carrying the disease) and unleashing them on the room. "I brought some. Here, I'll let them roam around. There is no reason only poor people should have the experience." That was certainly unusual AND memorable!

You can also present something unexpected or mysterious. The audience is then dependent on you to solve the mystery.

## Uncertainty

Arouse curiosity. Start your story, but leave the audience hanging until you finish it later. Or use a picture that makes people wonder what will happen next.

## Create a sense of antagonism

Present your topic as a great struggle, an epic journey that must be undertaken:

> It was me against the money hungry, fee-crazy airlines. I decided to play their game and win. NO! I will not pay baggage fees! I wore all my clothes on the plane. NO! I will not pay for a snack! I brought an apple, a peanut butter sandwich and a one-pound bag of peanut M&Ms. NO! I won't pay for a beverage!

*I brought an empty water bottle through security and filled it at a water fountain before boarding the plane. Victory was mine!*

## Keep the audience wanting more

Give them less and hold back information, making the audience reliant on you to connect the dots or finish the story. This may include requiring the audience to follow up with you in some fashion, like registering to receive a white paper/tool/ticket, going to a website to access information, etc.

## Use metaphors

Metaphors compare one thing to another: a presentation is a journey. Pat Benatar gave us "love is a battlefield." "Our family tree has deep roots, a sturdy trunk, lots of branches and a few nuts." Good metaphors are easy to remember and can often carry your message throughout the presentation.

## Use contrast

The opposite of a metaphor is telling the audience what something is not. "This is not rocket science," for example.

## Use comparisons

Our brains love making comparisons, and they can be an effective way to appeal to both logic and emotion. One way to influence through comparisons is to present your alternatives in the good-better-best framework. Sears invented this concept. They offer products (tools, appliances, etc.) at three different levels of quality, knowing that different buyer groups have different preferences in price and quality.

Savvy restaurateurs have one big-ticket item on the menu, knowing that this will attract a few diners. What this high-priced dish really does is drive customers to choose the item priced just below this one. Some restaurants even list the highest-priced item first on the menu to serve as an anchor against which we compare other prices. Everything after the most expensive item seems more reasonable. Your takeaway: position your alternatives so that you influence the audience's choice. Start with an option that is more extreme than the one you want your audience to select. By comparison, your preferred option looks better.

Another comparison technique is the tried-and-true before-and-after picture. Use this to show how your approach can make a discernable difference over the status quo. You can also incorporate a metaphor with your before and after.

Photos courtesy of TheEstateofThings.com

## Limit the number of options

Most of us have a limited capacity for remembering long lists. The psychological theory known as *the paradox of choice* says that the more options we have, the more anxiety we feel. To avoid creating anxiety in your audience—and to influence the outcomes or choices you prefer—limit the number of options you provide.

## Create a Mnemonic

Mnemonics are any learning techniques that aid in retaining information. Come up with a simple device or tool that helps your audience remember your key points. One of the first mnemonics I recall learning as a kid was an acronym for the colors of the rainbow:

**Roy G. Biv**     Red Orange Yellow Green
Blue Indigo Violet

Here are several other mnemonics you may remember (pun intended):

Lefty loosey, righty tighty
Red sky in the morning, sailors take warning
Red sky at night, sailors delight

In their book, *Made to Stick*, brothers Chip and Dan Heath provide their SUCCESs mnemonic for creating stickiness:

**S**imple is better than complex: focus on one key message
**U**nexpected trumps the usual pattern
**C**oncrete is better than abstract
**C**redible is better than vague or uncertain
**E**motions work better than dry and factual
**S**tories are easily remembered

In addition to using a great mnemonic, many of the sticky ideas in their book are useful for influential business presentations.

# Harness the power of framing

In addition to structuring for clarity and memorability and using sticky content, framing is a powerful tool to leverage your influence. Framing is the concept of presenting an idea in a way that will encourage your audience to accept your presentation premise.

One framing strategy is to utilize the concept of loss aversion described above. By framing a concept from the loss perspective, people are motivated to find a solution to avoid the loss, for example:

> *If we continue on the same path, we can realistically expect that we will experience a 17% decline in customer retention. By implementing the Gold Standard Service plan, we can reasonably expect to achieve customer retention rates in the 5 to 7% range.*

Another framing approach is to present your content in a way that elicits a desired emotion. Your choice of words, examples and delivery can all combine to do this. Emotions you might want your audience to feel include:

| | | | | |
|---|---|---|---|---|
| Hopeful | Excited | Surprised | Energized | Committed |
| Curious | Angry | Sad | Enthused | Happy |
| Justified | Decisive | Fear | Motivated | Disgust |

Here is an example of a frame intended to generate enthusiasm and motivation:

> *These market research findings prove that there is a large, needy, underserved market segment waiting for a solution. Our R&D group has a cost-effective solution that meets the target audience needs. Manufacturing has capacity to put this into production by the end of*

*the quarter. We can have a product on the market in 4 months. By authorizing this investment, we can beat the competition to market and tap into a $400 million opportunity. The revenue potential from this market segment could mean the difference between barely making our annual plan and exceeding it by more than 10 percent.*

In Susan Z. Finerty's book, *The Cross-Functional Influence Playbook*, she shares four key framing concepts that can be applied to influence in business presentations.

## Frame the issue in a way that is meaningful to your audience

Take the perspective of your audience. Use language and examples that are meaningful to them.

*Amazon started as an online bookstore. It proved its business model and then leveraged that to grow exponentially by adding product categories beyond books. We're doing the same thing. We've proven our business model of identifying cost savings in commercial construction. Like Amazon, we can leverage our model expertise to penetrate residential construction next. After that, we can move into adjacent markets to grow by capitalizing on the core competencies in our business model.*

## Frame in a larger context

Create a frame that helps your audience see how your issues relate to the bigger picture. How will this affect the way things are done now?

*Technology is allowing us to reach markets that we were previously unable to reach. We can now increase our market to compete successfully in Europe and South America. By investing in these technologies, we have the potential to double the size of our company over the next five years.*

## Be specific

Be specific about what you want the audience to know, feel and/or do.

*I am looking for your support in presenting this idea to the senior leadership committee on our department's behalf. I hope you are as excited as I am about the potential that this represents for our department.*

## Frame objectively

Be sure you create a frame that is free from bias and is supported by facts.

*None of us want to make cuts in our budgets, but we can all agree that reduced revenue means reduced spending.*

## Summary of Key Ideas

- Structure is critical for helping your audience remember your presentation.

- Structure with an introduction, body and conclusion.

- The conclusion is the most important part of your presentation. The last thing the audience hears, sees and feels will most strongly influence them. Don't leave your influence to chance. Begin your presentation design by focusing on your conclusion.

- The introduction is the second most important part of your presentation. It is important because it must capture attention, connect with the audience and establish your credibility. Work on the introduction second.

- The body is where you lay out the evidence that supports your presentation objective. Less is more. The most memorable presentations focus on just three main points.

- Use a compelling story to connect emotionally and memorably with your audience.

- Outline your presentation before you create it in your slide deck.

- Make your content "sticky" by using a variety of the techniques that make it easy for your audience to remember your points.

- Frame your presentation in a way that is meaningful to your audience. One way to do this is to use a big picture frame that helps the audience see the situation relative to a different perspective than they normally would. Be specific and be sure you frame objectively, avoiding bias.

## Put This to Work

1. Draft the conclusion of your presentation

2. Draft the introduction of your presentation

3. Outline the main points and their supporting subpoints that you will include in the body of your presentation

4. Which techniques will you use to increase the stickiness of your presentation?

5. How can you frame your presentation to increase your influence with this audience?

## Resources

Simon Sinek, "How Great Leaders Inspire Action" TED Talk, 2010.

Chip and Dan Heath, *Made to Stick*, 2007

Susan Z. Finerty, *The Cross-Functional Influence Playbook*, 2016

# CHAPTER 5

# Harness the Power of Stories

Stories can be one of the most compelling ways to influence your audience, but the wrong stories or the wrong timing can do more harm than good. It takes careful design and practice to use stories to their maximal effect.

*Ryan was not your stereotypical brainy IT guy. Sure, he had earned his degree from a great university. Yes, he had worked for an industry-leading Fortune 100 company and gained incredible experience. But it was obvious to us when he introduced himself to the class that Ryan was an extrovert who would enjoy improving his presentation skills in this workshop.*

*Ryan quickly embraced the idea of using stories in his presentation. Oddly though, they didn't work for him. His natural style involved TMI (too much information)—way too much! His attempts at telling one story always seemed to intersect with other stories. He layered context on top of context until it was hard to remember where he started, where he was going or why it mattered. Whereas great stories include just enough specifics to make sense, they never* include every possible relevant fact. And they aren't stories for the sake of stories—as with everything in your presentation, the stories need to support your objective.

Only a few minutes into Ryan's presentation, you could see in the audience body language that the hoped-for connection hadn't been made. They had lost interest. Ryan could see this as well, and his response was to inject more energy and talk faster, with greater emphasis, which didn't help.

We coached Ryan to choose one story and to provide only as many details as necessary for the audience to get the picture. By providing fewer specifics, shortening his story and using fewer words, the next time he presented, Ryan captured attention and increased his credibility with his story, rather than losing the audience in the weeds.

## Why Stories Work

Why are stories so effective in presentations? There are a few different factors in play that help make storytelling so powerfully influential:

- Stories break audience preoccupation to capture attention

- Stories trigger chemical responses from the brain that can help you engage the audience

- The magic of well-designed stories can cross generational gaps and cultural boundaries

## Stories serve as memorable mental snapshots

## Do You Have A Minute?

Barely. Our brains treat attention as a scarce resource. We do not want to give this resource away. Due to the digital nature of modern life, the brain is assaulted almost every second by multiple messages. Just having a cellphone in visual range cues the brain to be on alert for incoming (possibly important) messages. You, as presenter, must compete with very powerful forces over which you have almost no control. This chapter illustrates how you can achieve just that using the power of storytelling.

You need to say or do something to interrupt where people are at that moment focusing their attention and to draw it to you. The old norms of an audience giving the presenter some time to get going have changed. If something does not immediately grab their attention, their thoughts will very quickly go back to their own problems, the next thing on their mental schedule. These days, it is a big mistake to use your first few minutes to tell them who you are, your title and tenure, something about your organization, who asked you to speak, what the topic is and how happy or grateful you are to be there.

What you need to do is give the audience something beautiful to see, something remarkable to think about, something unexpected. Give them something that takes them away from their immediate concerns, so they are eager to hear what you're going to say or show them next.

## The Name Is Bond, James Bond

For the past 55 years, producers have created James Bond films that grab their audiences with a formula that still works today. The opening scene is usually at least five minutes of amazing action. The audience does not know or care yet about the plot or characters; they are simply mesmerized with the incredible car chases, airplane or helicopter stunts and desperate hand-to-hand fighting. Explosions, fires, fatal falls and unexpected escapes litter those first few minutes of every Bond flick. The audience is transported into another world and happily stays with Bond until he saves the day.

Many TED talks use the same formula. The speaker gives the audience something outside their normal world by showing or telling them a story. The drama, humor or even pathos breaks their preoccupation with their own lives and gives the presenter time to engage them in the presentation. Like a movie production, influential business presentation stories are NOT off-the-cuff. The story is well thought through. It is designed to fit the presentation objective, and it grabs attention and elicits specific emotions in the audience. And like a movie scene, it is rehearsed until it can be done very well.

When the vulnerable and trusted actor in the story overcomes some or all of the challenges thrown at them by hard work, persevering through painful experiences and doing those difficult things that build character, the audience celebrates with them. Even if things don't turn out perfectly, the story leads the audience to have empathy, maybe even sympathy for its hero.

Telling a real story from your life can have a particularly strong impact on an audience. The storyteller becomes vulnerable by revealing challenges, weaknesses, disappointments, hardships—real experiences to which the audience may relate. We tend to trust people who reveal things about their character and life that are not perfect. The emotional connections made by telling a story create a much stronger memory than using reason and logic alone.

## Work with Brain Chemistry

Beginning with a story avoids the mundane information dump that audiences have come to expect. A good story can influence the brain to release a neurochemical called oxytocin, which signals that it is safe to allow another person to approach. Oxytocin seems to enhance empathy and even motivate people to engage in cooperative behaviors, such as listening and giving attention.

Our brains produce oxytocin in response to stories that engage, that override the need to attend to other pressing needs. Therefore, the story must be compelling, not just a series of connected factual events. Great stories have an emotional component in order to trigger the oxytocin response and drive below the consciousness level. Therefore, the best stories develop some tension, a feeling that something has gone or might go wrong, and that there is risk involved. Then our brains relate at both the conscious and subconscious levels.

A story that is totally predictable does not contain these elements and generally won't produce the desired response.

# Turn good stories into great storytelling

Powerful stories don't just happen—they're the result of hard work and experimentation. To tell a compelling story, it's necessary to understand the elements that go into creating one. There are countless ways to approach telling a story, but we've limited our comments to three influential types:

*Chronological*: The *past* leads to the *present* which leads to the *future*

*Results-Focused*: The *problem* leads to the *solution* which leads to *results*

*MacGyver Approach*: The *what* leads to *so what* which leads to the *what now*

Stories, plays and movies have a three-stage structure with a beginning, a middle and an ending. The *Set-up* corresponds to the beginning; the *Confrontation* corresponds to the middle; and the *Resolution* corresponds to the end. Storytellers have been using this structure at least since Aristotle wrote it down in 335 B.C.

## The Unforgettable Start

No matter which story type is used, your story set-up must be sharp. Characters are introduced. We quickly discover who are heroes, who are villains, and we learn what we need to know about their world and times. Somebody creates a conflict by causing a problem for others. The problem must resonate with the audience.

## The Hero or Enemy Must Deserve Attention

The characters do not all have to be human; the *Set-up* can be to play the villain of disease against the hero of a patient or scientific investigator. It could be a competitor who takes advantage of customers by over-promising and under-delivering. We just need to know who is in the story and why we should root for or against them.

Steve Jobs liked to make Apple the good guys and competitors the villains. Even if the real situation is complex, make the initial effort to describe it easy to quickly understand. You can get back to complications later if they are really important. Your objective is to grab attention, not to do everything possible to hold onto it.

When you can create a connection between your audience and the good guys, do it. People love to imagine themselves doing what the hero or winner in the story does. It creates empathy, which gets sent your way as a benefit.

## Details Create Drama, Which Feeds Emotions

As the designer of the *Set-up*, you need to judiciously figure out how much detail to feed the audience at this moment. Too much detail weighs the scene down, slows progress and raises too many questions. You really don't want your audience to interrupt you now. Bringing in the right kind of specific information that supports the danger or opportunity of the scene is your objective.

For example, it is one thing to say that "about 10 percent of all healthcare costs in the U.S. are wasted." While that doesn't sound great, it doesn't sound horrible. We all waste resources. We expect giant organizations to have a certain amount of inefficiency. It is something very different to say that "every year nearly $1.7 trillion, yes trillion with a T, is wasted in the U.S. on unnecessary operations, tests and medicines." You can then add another dramatic statement of comparison, such as, "That is as much waste as the value of everything, all goods and services produced in an entire year, in a big country like Russia, with about 144 million people." You hope to challenge the status quo in peoples' minds, to get them to say, "I didn't know that," "That's a different way of putting it," "I want to know more."

## The Middle: Surprises Are Your Friends

As with great movies, your story should not be perfectly predictable. If you appear too predictable, your audience races ahead to your logical conclusion, and they stop listening carefully.

Your design should include places where the hero unexpectedly almost loses or the villain almost wins. This can happen in the *Set-up* but generally works better in the *Confrontation*. This is where the hero's world is turned upside-down. The hero must change, learn or fail. This is exciting stuff, and you need to convey to the audience what risks, efforts, failures, false-starts and reversals took place. Too many speakers zip past this, especially when telling personal stories, thinking that they don't want to blow their own horn too much. You need to master the concept that only within danger lies worthwhile success.

Your job as presenter is to show that danger, those difficulties, in ways that the audience can appreciate and empathize with. When you expose an obstacle, take enjoyment in showing how by taking an unexpected route, you or your team or the hero, who may have been nervous, scared or lacked confidence and certainty, stepped forward anyway. The audience will interpret that as courage, not phony bluster. However, be careful not to introduce everything as a surprise; the audience will buy only so many of them.

## Stories Finish Well—They Don't Just End

In the *Resolution*, you will need to show how you, the team or the hero moved past all the obstacles in the *Confrontation* and resolved the problem from the *Set-up*. You need to show the audience how everything turned out. While they may believe that you solved the problem due to the fine presentation of logic, facts and statistics, you want them to leave feeling that this was a satisfying ending, not just an ending. This is true no matter which story type you chose. For a business problem in a results-focused type of story, the results need to have been tested against the business parameters they were supposed to achieve, such as profit, usability, reliability, longevity, serviceability, customer acceptance and adoption.

# The Chronological Story

Simon Sinek's TED talk, "How Great Leaders Inspire Action," uses three very different stories to help drive home his key points. The first is about the Wright brothers' invention of the airplane, and it has a simple chronological structure.

*The Past*: Sinek benefits from the basic familiarity everyone in the United States has with this story. Therefore, he provides only a brief introduction, mostly to say that the Wright brothers were not wealthy or famous, nor did they have the backing of any powerful organizations. We all suspected as much.

He then introduces us to an unfamiliar character, Samuel Pierpont Langley, a wealthy, very well-connected man who also wanted to invent the airplane. Each time he mentions Langley, he uses his full, somewhat pretentious-sounding name. He notes that in contrast to the Wrights investing their own very limited funds as bicycle makers, Langley had been given $50,000 by the United States government's War Department to invent the plane—about $1.45 million in today's dollars.

*The Present*: This centers on what the Wright brothers were doing right around the time they completed their famous flight. Sinek notes a few interesting facts about their daily construction and testing struggles. He contrasts their home-grown efforts and lack of formal education to Langley being able to hire the best and brightest, buy first-rate materials and receive coverage from the *New York Times*.

Of course, the Wright brothers persevered until they created a functioning machine. Langley quit trying when he heard that the Wrights had succeeded. Sinek then makes his point: the Wrights knew their *why*—the motivation behind all their effort.

*The Future*: The Wrights had a vision for the future of mankind benefitting from their success in bringing controlled flight to the world. Sinek claims that Langley, instead, only wanted success so he could become wealthier and more famous. Sinek is able to leave the story at this point because he can safely assume that most people would agree that the Wrights' future is the one that happened. He succeeded in using the story to reinforce his point that great leaders are those who start with "why," because they are the people who are able to inspire those around them.

## The Results-Focused Story

The results-focused structure is a bit like the James Bond approach. The story starts with a big problem that needs to be resolved. But before presenting the solution, it's important to make sure the audience is emotionally involved in the problem. Make it real using colorful language, perhaps a picture, compelling statistics. This is how you hook the audience. They want to stay tuned to find out how you will fix the problem.

The solution, as revealed by the story, then becomes the focus of your presentation.

But the solution isn't what's most important in an influential presentation: the result of the solution is how you gain audience commitment and achieve your presentation objective. The result is the *which means that* piece that makes it clear to the audience how they will benefit; the outcome they can expect personally from your solution.

Here is how one of our workshop participants used the results-focused structure:

*If you know anyone who has gone through cancer, then you've seen what that diagnosis can do to people physically and emotionally. I know because I watched my mother fall apart after her diagnosis. She was overwhelmed. Confused by foreign-sounding medical terminology. A second medical opinion differed from the first. A third contradicted the first two. She felt like the clock was ticking and she needed to make a decision. Yet she seemed paralyzed. Afraid. She told me her world felt like it was "out of control."*

*That's the problem with so many cancer diagnoses. Patients must make critical treatment decisions, often under the gun, at a time when they are psychologically and emotionally most fragile.*

Yet there are new approaches that provide the physician and the patient with personalized, definitive results that help them make more informed decisions based on the patient's situation rather than on a large study of patients with characteristics LIKE theirs.

In the next 20 minutes, I want to share with you how genomic assays are helping cancer patients. I want you to learn how you can play a role in the advancement of this approach. You can be a part of the solution. The result of genomic assays is that patients have the information they need to make informed decisions and gain peace of mind.

## The MacGyver Story

Stories of discovery, overcoming the odds or making lemonade out of lemons fit pretty well with the MacGyver structural approach. Legendary golfer Ray Floyd tells a fascinating MacGyver-style story about traveling to a small, run-down course in West Texas to play a poor Mexican kid. He introduces the *What* phase by describing how he was at the top of his game, had just won some tournaments and enjoyed gambling, especially on himself. He talks about how a friend talked him into betting on his ability to beat an unknown Mexican kid who picked up golf balls on the driving range and had only won a few local tournaments, nothing big.

We move to the *So What* phase, when they meet on the kid's home territory, a beat-up, dry, desert course with lots of West Texas wind as a complicating factor. Floyd describes the match and his opponent's unexpected play. While they are both under par and playing extremely well, he loses by one stroke. That gets him fired up for a rematch. It's one thing to beat a champion golfer once, on your home course, when he doesn't expect it. But now fully prepared, Floyd still lost the rematch—again by one stroke.

He is forced to move on to the *What Now* phase. Some of you may have guessed that the Mexican kid was Lee Trevino, a self-taught master of gamesmanship on the golf course. Trevino went on to win 58 professional tournaments and is now in the World Golf Hall of Fame, along with Floyd. Ray had to admit when he'd been whipped and put his pride in his pocket until he won his next tournament.

This story does not take long to tell, but when told well, it is one that will stick with you the rest of your life. There is something wonderful about the underdog winning, the experience of the old pro versus the new kid on the block, that makes this MacGyver approach work well. Many experiences that include some sort of life lessons could be structured with the MacGyver approach to create memorable stories.

And the MacGyver approach doesn't just apply to stories—it can structure an entire presentation. Steve Jobs was a master of using the MacGyver structure to capture interest, generate enthusiasm and lead the audience where he wanted them to go.

In 2001, Jobs introduced the iPod—you can watch his presentation on YouTube. Jobs did not introduce Apple's interest in taking over the music publishing world and then show the tools that would accomplish this goal (although that's what Apple has done). He took the *What* state of the individual listener to digital music and described all the problems of that state. From Apple's point of view, one critical factor was that there was no market leader. No one had figured out the recipe for how to best reach the individual listener. The *So What* aspects were all the implications of the *What* state. He discussed all of the then-current technologies and their strengths and weaknesses. Those alternatives are all shown to be amazingly inferior to the iPod capabilities, the *What Now*, which he discusses at length.

This formula does not take a lot of time, it condenses a lot of information, and it quickly moves the audience to the *What Now* state, which is where Jobs wanted this to go in the first place. When you are trying to influence people to accept a new idea, telling them in an apparently honest and open fashion about the *What* state is a great way to get attention, to get people nodding their heads, to help them see what is wrong with the status quo. They are led to understand that you get it, that you see things their way.

The *What Now* discussion takes control of what their alternatives are and enables you to structure the arguments for and against something. This builds credibility, if and only if you are clever and knowledgeable about the subject.

MacGyver was always resourceful, reacted quickly and creatively to changing circumstances and often came up with a solution that straight-line reasoning might not find. He would set you up for the action to follow with a relatively short *What* phase of the story. There were always things blowing up during the *So What* phase of the show, so he had to do the unexpected. People love surprises and the unexpected elements of stories. After that, the *What Now* phase of the story can end more calmly, with a rational "I should have seen than coming" conclusion.

## Personal Story Sources

Workshop participants often struggle with including stories claiming they have no interesting stories. Here are a few story sources to get your creative juices flowing:

- Times in your life (childhood, college, young adulthood, etc.)

- Interesting or unexpected experiences

- Relatives who have influenced you

- Struggles you or others have overcome

- Authority figures (scientific, current, historic, etc.)

- Admired peers / colleagues

- How you were inspired to pursue your profession

- Things you cherish (relationships, awards, special places, successes, etc.)

- Things that have harmed you or others (disease, accidents, etc.)

- Events/people that challenged you (time wasted on efforts that went nowhere, awful professors, absurdly demanding customers, etc.)

Be sure that the story you choose vividly and compellingly supports your presentation objective.

What's your story?

The underlying concepts of clear, concise and compelling apply to storytelling as well. The story must clearly tie in to your objective—there should be no room for guesswork as to how the story is relevant to the rest of your presentation. The story must unfold quickly to avoid losing audience interest. And finally, the story must appeal to the audience. This ties in with knowing your audience—how likely are they to relate to the situation or characters?

## Test Your Story

There are some important caveats and cautions to consider when telling a story.

Naturally, all stories should be practiced so that they come across as intended. But personal stories should be tested with another person so that you can be sure you can deliver it as intended. We have seen a number of people become overly emotional when telling a difficult or personal story. They are clearly uncomfortable, and the audience usually becomes uncomfortable too. Then, the focus becomes the speaker rather than the objective of the story.

This also happens with humor occasionally. The speaker finds their story so funny that they can't complete it, and again, the audience reacts to the behavior of the speaker rather than the story. Practice telling the entire story, with emphasis on the timing, word emphasis and pauses that make humor work.

Test your story with the following questions:

1. *Does the story support your presentation objective?* Being remembered as a good storyteller is great as long as you move the presentation forward. We've seen presenters get so involved in the story that they are remembered as entertainers, not presenters.

2. *Does the story include enough detail to be compelling without overwhelming the audience?* Include just enough details and context but don't drown the audience in unnecessary information. You need to make sure the story is simple enough to drive your points home without needing to educate the audience for several minutes so they can understand it. This annoys many people, distracts others and can turn the positive emotions you were hoping for into negatives.

3. *Is the story complete?* Test your story to ensure it is complete enough to accomplish its objectives. Gaps in time, logic or even content will be exposed if your trial listener has to ask basic questions in order to understand the story. This can happen when the speaker knows the story so well that they skip something that they think they've said already.

4. *Are all the facts correct?* Getting a name, date, quote or important fact wrong can stop the audience from hearing what comes next. You've

broken your nonverbal agreement to be truthful and accurate. They are counting on you to have done your research, and if you fail them, you lose their trust. You don't want the audience to stop listening before you've finished telling the story just because you did not get a simple fact right.

5. *Is your story unique?* Some stories have passed their expiration date. They've been told too often to have any positive effect. No one on the planet needs to hear the story of the starfish on the beach again. If you need to reference some famous event, put a different twist on it. Show your audience they were worth the additional effort to reframe and rethink this well-known story.

6. *Does your humor work with the audience?* Humorous stories can work wonders on the audience, but they need to be tested. They may not be nearly as funny as you think they are. Your delivery may not work. They may unintentionally offend some of the audience. They may seem silly rather than funny and thereby detract from your presentation. Jokes are risky unless well vetted. Off-color jokes generally make you seem unprofessional, even if they are funny. Test, test, test.

Remember, the only reason your story is valuable is because it can influence the audience. You use it to help them understand how your introduction, main points or conclusion are relevant and meaningful. Designed well, your story increases the audience's willingness to listen, to try to understand you, to have empathy for your situation and to stick with you.

## Summary of Key Ideas

- Stories are a powerful way to break audience preoccupation and connect emotionally and memorably.

- Stories trigger chemical responses from the brain that can help you engage the audience.

- The magic of well-designed stories can cross generational gaps and cultural boundaries.

- Three effective story structures are:

  Chronological: The past leads to the present which leads to the future

  Results-Focused: The problem leads to the solution, which leads to results

  MacGyver Approach: The *What* leads to *So What*, which leads to *What Now*

- Memorable stories have three parts:

  The *Set-up* corresponds to the beginning

  The *Confrontation* corresponds to the middle

  The *Resolution* corresponds to the end

- Be sure your story starts unforgettably and includes only as many specifics as necessary to capture attention. Avoid the tendency to get into too much detail in the beginning of your story.

- Test your story with the following questions:

  Does the story support your presentation objective?

Does the story include enough detail to be compelling without overwhelming the audience?

Is the story complete?

Are all the facts correct?

Is your story unique?

Does your humor work with the audience?

## Put this to work

1. Think of a story that you can use to support your presentation. Capture that story in a few bullet points.

2. Pick one of the story structures, and fill in your story parts:

   *The Set-up*

   *The Confrontation*

   *The Resolution*

3. What will you include in the beginning to start unforgettably?

4. Now test your story with a few colleagues. Incorporate their feedback and re-test.

## Resources

Steve Jobs iPod launch, Apple Music Event 2001, various recordings available at www.youtube.com

# CHAPTER 6

# Design Powerful Slide Decks

The slide deck is the core of modern presentations, but the heart of an influential presentation is the connection you make with the audience, not the content of your slides. Clear and concise are the key words to think about here. Your slides should encourage the audience to focus on your words, not distract from them.

*Ashley was a newly minted engineering PhD attending our presentation skills workshop. Her first attempt at an introduction for her presentation was an engineering miracle. She stuffed more technical information into four minutes than anyone thought possible. She definitely created an impression—but not a positive one.*

*Ashley's introduction had 12 complex slides packed with information. No pictures, no story and, from my observation of body language in the audience, no interest. Her delivery was driven, dry and dull. Her slides took an ambitious objective and blew it up until the presentation collapsed under its own weight*

*I had spoken with Ashley before class and learned that this was her first opportunity to learn how* to present in a business setting. Her previous presentations were academic. She was a bit stunned to learn that the academic methodology she had seen and been expected to master was dead wrong for a business setting. But her sincere interest in learning was apparent in the way she took on feedback from us and her peers in the class.

At the end of day one, participants were instructed to rework their presentations and told them they would have the opportunity to present them again the next morning. Many people tweak their work and spend most of their effort improving their delivery, but not Ashley. Like no one I'd seen before, Ashley revised her presentation objective and trashed her first slide deck. She simplified her slides, replaced pie charts with pictures, added real-world examples, eliminated annoying animation and made herself the center of attention. Her deck looked like that of an old pro. This transformation was a great start to the second day of the workshop.

## Rethink your presentation priorities

It is often said that people spend more time planning a vacation than they do planning their retirement. A similar comparison can be made for the amount of time spent creating a slide deck versus time spent creating the presentation. The star of the presentation is you, not your slide deck. Yet many people labor over their decks, spending hours searching for the perfect images and rearranging each slide. And sadly, too many labor-intensive presentation decks fail to support the objective or influence the desired outcome.

This chapter lays out common pitfalls to avoid and simple tricks to improve audience response to your presentation and get you to your influence objective. The good news is that these techniques can actually reduce the time spent working on slides and help you present more confidently.

Rethink your presentation priorities. Focus first on your presentation objective and main points. Make sure your points are compelling and persuasive. Add your subpoints and proof. Arrange and re-arrange the itinerary for the journey you will take with your audience. Identify the best ways to influence your audience with sticky content.

*Then—and only then—work on your deck.*

Most of the presenters we work with will never give a TED talk. Creating TED-worthy slides takes days and a lot of professional support. Few of our clients have the need, bandwidth, skills or budget for such presentations.

The resources available for slide deck creation are increasing every day. There are blogs, books, presentation software and websites galore that can consume your precious time. Expensive design firms abound that claim they can transform your content into award-winning decks. And for some critically important presentations, the investment may be worth it. For most presentations, however, striving for perfection will cost more than it is worth in time and money.

Yes, your deck is important. It is a reflection of you. Slides can contribute to being influential, and they can definitely block influence if done poorly. But they are just a tool. Use them to logically support your content, plant memorable images and create emotion. Perfect your deck but avoid striving for perfection—you don't have time for that.

## Common Pitfalls

There are four common mistakes people make when preparing their presentations. These mistakes not only limit effectiveness, they tend to waste time in preparation.

### Creating your presentation while creating your deck

An architect doesn't design the house while she's building it. And neither should you design your presentation while creating your deck. Be disciplined about following the content design strategies laid out in chapter 4 and start with an outline.

### Thinking of your deck as a receptacle for all the information you want to remember during your presentation

We've heard many people tell us that they use their slide deck as their safety net. They include too many words for every point they want to make so they won't forget anything.

Instead of over-stuffing every slide, capture your one key idea for each slide in the notes section underneath it. Then, present in the mode that allows you to see your current slide, your notes for that slide and the next slide in the deck (in PowerPoint, go to Slide Show and click Use Presenter View). This way, the audience doesn't need to see your safety net.

*Capture your one key idea in the notes section*

## Using your deck as a handout

Many people in our workshops tell us that the reason they include so much content on each slide is because they print out the deck to use as a handout. They feel they need to include lots of information so the deck makes sense after the presentation. When your slides are designed appropriately to reinforce your words, the slides themselves will not stand alone.

A slide deck is not a document. If you must provide a handout, consider doing the following:

1. Use your presentation outline; this framework includes your structure and main points

2. Write a brief synopsis of your presentation

3. Write a white paper

4. Copy and paste each slide into a Word document and include the key point for each slide

5. Print slides with notes

And no matter what type of handout you use, if practical, do not distribute it before your presentation. You will lose your audience as they turn their attention to reviewing the printed material.

## Limiting your deck to a small number of slides

Minimizing the number of slides in your deck will most likely cause you to add too much information to each slide. Remember: there is no cost per slide to worry about! And if you keep to the *one point per slide* rule, you will naturally need more slides. Using more slides and changing the audience's view more frequently actually encourages increased attention.

## Twelve power tips for deck design

The following tips are the ones we find ourselves repeating from workshop to workshop to help participants create compelling and influential slide decks. To maintain audience attention, use the following guidelines:

## Think of your slides as billboards

A well-designed billboard can be understood in a 3-second glance as you drive down the interstate. If your slide is too complicated to be understood in 3 seconds, break it down to multiple slides. Good billboards and slides...

- are easy to comprehend quickly
- use compelling, simple images
- have a minimal number of words

## One point per slide

Don't try to cram too much on one slide. We recommend the *one point per slide* rule of thumb. Break complex concepts into multiple points, one per slide.

## Optimize canvas white space

To minimize clutter and enhance clarity, start with a minimalist template. The trend is away from using slide titles. Instead, create the equivalent of a title in a box used consistently where needed. Then add minimal text and or graphics, keeping the slide clean and uncluttered.

Research and common sense reveal that people immediately reject overcrowded slides. This puts a negative spin on those slides: two or three over-stuffed slides could lead to such a negative impression that you may not recover.

*A note on working with templates*: Many of our clients are required to use company templates for presentations. Sadly, many of the templates are not well designed, taking up precious canvas space and forcing the use of titles on each slide. If your company has a template, check with the powers that be to see how much latitude you have in adjusting the template to create maximum white space.

## Use headlines instead of titles

Don't make your audience work for your key idea: deliver it as a headline. Titles are nice. Headlines capture attention and drive home your one key idea for that slide.

## Minimize builds and animation

Using a build allows you to add information, whether images or text, in order to direct the audience's attention as you go. Doing this too often, however, can be distracting. Use builds when necessary to break down a complex slide into components that you reveal as you describe the concept.

Also use animation sparingly. The animation feature can be helpful to draw attention to a key point, but over-use of animation may give the impression of a less-than-professional design.

## Replace words with graphics

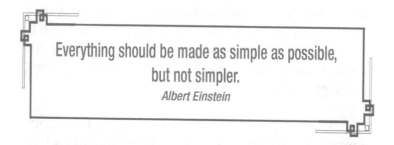

> Everything should be made as simple as possible, but not simpler.
> *Albert Einstein*

Lists of bullet points are a sure way to lose your audience, as they stop listening to you so they can quickly read what it will take you longer to say. You have given them permission to jump ahead, which gets you out of sync with your audience.

Instead of words, use visual markers: pictures, images, graphics. These are much more memorable and, when used appropriately, almost act as a filing system for your ideas in the minds of your audience.

When selecting graphics and pictures, be sure the image resolution is high enough for the size of the room where you will be presenting.

## A cautionary note about permission

When selecting graphics and photos, be sure you have proper permission. While there are millions of images available on Google, many require specific permission for you to use legally. If you are not sure whether an image is free to use, it is best to leave it out and select one which is. And simply adding an attribution to an image does not necessarily protect you legally.

Images that are legally free to use are free from copyright restrictions or are licensed under creative commons public domain dedication. According to CreativeCommons.org, such status means that "the person who associated a work with this deed has dedicated the work to the public domain by waiving all of his or her rights to the work worldwide under copyright law, including all related and neighboring rights, to the extent allowed by law. You can copy, modify, distribute and perform the work, even for commercial purposes, all without asking permission."

So what are your options?

- Consider purchasing images from sources such as iStock, Shutterstock or Getty Images.

- Select images from one of the many websites that specialize in free stock photos. We've included some sources at the end of this chapter.

- Create your own images.

## Incorporate short videos

Videos are a great way to add variety to your presentation. They are often the best way to demonstrate certain points or concepts. And because video is multisensory, people naturally tune in. For the highest engagement and retention, keep videos short—preferably around 30-60 seconds.

While professionally produced video clips are great, even rough-around-the-edges video edited from your smart phone can capture interest and be influential. Be sure any video you use quickly and clearly makes the point you are intending.

File any video you use on your computer and insert it directly into your deck. Never rely on Wi-Fi to access a video. From personal experience, we can tell you that Murphy's Law is alive and well and will cause a mess if you attempt to stream your video!

## Pull out specifics on data-heavy slides

Sometimes there is no way around including a spreadsheet or a slide with lots of data. Presenting monthly financials, research results, analyses... these all require data. Make it easy for your audience to focus on what is important by using one of the following techniques:

- Insert a large, colorful arrow that points to the data you are referencing.

- Use a circle to highlight key data.

- Make a screenshot of the slide, then crop to the data you want to feature. Save the cropped picture, copy/paste this into a slide, and expand to your preferred size. Add a border and animation so that the cropped data box "zooms" to the foreground.

- In Slide Show mode, use the zoom feature by clicking on the magnifying glass icon at the lower left corner of screen, highlighting the area you want to magnify, and then left-clicking. A right-click returns you to normal view.

- In Presentation mode, use the magnifying glass by clicking on the magnifying glass icon that will appear when pointing your mouse in the lower-left corner of the slide. Hover over the part of the slide you want to expand and left-click. To return to normal view, right-click.

| COST PER WEEK | | | TRAVEL | COST | TOTAL |
|---|---|---|---|---|---|
| Week 1 | SMF 1000 | $ | 3000 | $ 75,535 | $ 78,535 |
| Week 2 | SMF 2000 | $ | | | |
| Week 3 | SMF 3000 | $ | | | |
| Development | | | | | |

| | TOTAL | COST/PERSON |
|---|---|---|
| | $ 89,150 | $ 1,938 |
| | $ 92,880 | $ 1,106 |
| | $ 21,465 | $ 740 |
| | $ 20,000 | |
| | $ 9,000 | |
| | $ 232,495 | $ 1,462 |

| TOTAL COST ANALYSIS | | |
|---|---|---|
| PROGRAM | # DAYS | # PARTICIPA |
| SMF 1000 | 2.5 | 46 |
| SMF 2000 | 2 | 84 |
| SMF 3000 | 1 | 29 |
| Development | | |
| Travel | | |
| TOTAL | | 159 |

OLD WINEAUX, INC.
INCOME STATEMENT
FOR THE YEAR ENDED DECEMBER 31, 2020

| REVENUE: | |
|---|---|
| Sales | $ 1,480,000 |
| Interest revenue | 35,000 |
| Dividend revenue | 15,000 |
| Infrequent or unusual gains | 9,000 |
| Total revenue | 1,539,000 |
| EXPENSES: | |
| Cost of goods sold | 600,000 |
| Selling | 100,000 |
| Administrative | 220,000 |
| Interest expense | 15,000 |
| Infrequent or unusual losses | 4,000 |
| Total expenses | 939,000 |
| Income before income taxes | 600,000 |
| Income taxes | 208,000 |
| Income from continuing operations | 392,000 |
| Discontinue operations: | |
| Income from operations, less income tax of $24,80 | 54,000 |
| Loss on disposal, less income tax of $41,000 | (90,000) |
| Total discontinued operations | (36,000) |
| Income before extraordinary item | 356,000 |
| Extraordinary item, less income tax of $23,000 | (45,000) |
| Net income | $ 311,000 |

There are many other techniques to create a zoom effect that focuses on the most important data on the slide. If you'd like to spend more time on this, do a web search on how to create a zoom effect using your presentation software.

Knowing how to create focal points will distinguish you from the all-too-typical presenter who simply pastes up a complex spreadsheet or graph and then tries to use a shaky laser pointer to get the audience to see the important parts. Trying to follow a tiny dot across a busy slide can quickly become annoying for the audience. This is when people start asking for you to give them a copy of your slides. If you make the key information too difficult to follow, the audience gives up on following and only wants the data—and may stop listening to you altogether.

## Be consistent in your design

One of the reasons that slide templates are popular is that they create consistency with font styles and sizes, layout and color. If you are not using a template, it is important to be consistent with your design elements. Stick with one main font and perhaps one secondary font for contrast. Popular font styles for decks include Arial, Calibri, Garamond, Gill Sans MT and Rockwell.

Remember that sans-serif fonts (like Arial), which have no tiny lines to jazz up the style, are better for typical projector resolution projection than serif styles like Times New Roman. You don't want to strain the eyes of your audience as they follow along through a long presentation—another reason to use fewer words!

Popular font styles: **Arial**

Popular font styles: **Calibri**

Popular font styles: **Garamond**

Popular font styles: **Gil Sans MT**

Popular font styles: **Rockwell**

Keep your color palette to no more than 4–5 options. To try out different color combinations, use colourlovers. com or coolors.com, two websites that help you create your palette and look at palettes created by others.

Font size is another important element to keep in mind for design consistency. Use the same size font for your headline or title on each slide. The appropriate font size for each slide depends on what other elements are on the slide. Most experts agree that a minimum font size of 32 is the easiest for your audience to read. In general, make the size as large as possible while minimizing the amount of text on each slide.

When including text, use an active voice rather than passive:

Passive: The presentation was given by the product manager.

More active: The product manager gave the presentation.

*Note on reversed type:* Reversed type—the use of a light font on a dark background—can be dramatic and stand out. When overused, however, it can be distracting and even cause a perceived text "vibration." Use this style sparingly for making key points.

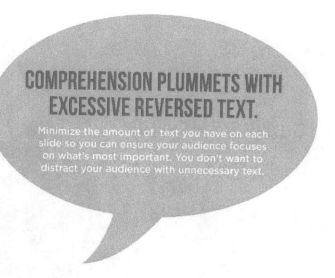

## Use slide layout

To help you with layout, turn on the gridlines feature in your presentation software. In PowerPoint, right-click on the slide, click on Grid and Guides in the box, then click on Display grid on screen. You now see a faint grid to help you line up and space your content. Note: The grid does not display in Present mode.

## Use full-bleed slides

Full-bleed, minimal-word slides, where the background image fills the entire slide, are impactful and dramatic. This style is effective for emphasizing your main points. To do this effectively, you will need a high-resolution image. If the image is too small, it will appear pixelated as you expand it to fit the slide. A good rule of thumb is to use images that are at least 1920 pixels wide and 1080 pixels high.

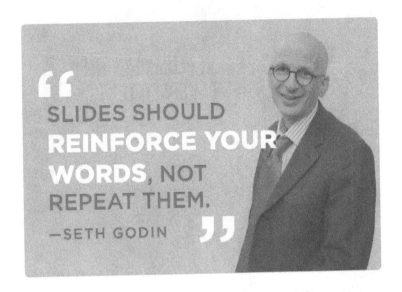

## Use slide sorter mode

Another way to assess your design and flow is to use your software's slide sorter view. This allows you to see many slides at one time. Scroll up and down to check for design congruity and flow. You can easily re-arrange slides this way.

## Summary of Key Ideas

- Develop your presentation objective and outline your presentation BEFORE creating your slide deck. Resist the temptation to create your presentation as you build your deck.

- Avoid the four common slide deck mistakes:
  1. Creating your presentation while creating your deck
  2. Thinking of your deck as a receptacle for all the information you want to remember during your presentation
  3. Using your deck as a handout
  4. Trying to keep your deck to a small number of slides

- Incorporate the 12 power tips for deck design:
  1. Think of your slides as billboards
  2. One point per slide
  3. Optimize canvas white space
  4. Use headlines instead of titles
  5. Minimize builds and animations
  6. Replace words with graphics and pictures
  7. Incorporate short videos
  8. Pull out specifics on data-heavy slides
  9. Be consistent in your design
  10. Use slide layout
  11. Use full bleed slides
  12. Use slide sorter mode

## Put This to Work

1. Open a presentation deck you've recently developed. Check to be sure that the deck does not include any of the common pitfalls. If you have made any of these mistakes, correct them now.

2. For that same presentation deck, how many of the 12 power tips do you use? Spend time now to incorporate additional power tips to make your presentation more influential.

## Resources

Microsoft PowerPoint Help Center: https://support.office.com/en-us/powerpoint

To purchase images: iStockPhoto.com, Shutterstock.com or Gettyimages.com

Links to 21 free stock photo websites: https://blog.snappa.com/free-stock-photos/

Color palette assistance: colourlovers.com or coolors.com

Fonts: Dafont.com, fontsquirrel.com, 1001fonts.com, whatfontis.com

Icons: Iconfinder.com

Deck design inspiration: Canva.com Video resources: videoscribe.com

Free master slide designs: brainybetty.com

# CHAPTER 7

# Deliver Influentially

Have you ever been in the audience and watched a presenter struggle to present? Most of us have suffered through this painful situation. My reactions to a struggling presenter go from annoyance to pity. Lack of preparation, failure to engage and read the audience and fear of public speaking can all contribute to a weak presentation. Even subject matter experts sometimes struggle, because it isn't just the content of a presentation that must be compelling, it's your presence on stage. But there are concrete steps anyone can take to improve their delivery skills.

*Emily had a golden opportunity to present her firm's unique capabilities to a room full of potential prospects. She has personally experienced incredible benefits from the products she represents. She is a believer and is proud to rep this line.*

*She spent the week before her presentation deciding what to share with the audience. She spent the night before going through the benefits of each product in her mind. She showed up early and arranged a display of products on a table. Emily was ready when she was introduced. But something went wrong.*

*Emily's nervousness was apparent to everyone in the room. It manifested itself in a quiet, quavering, almost apologetic voice. She presented while frozen in place in front of her display table. She made broad, sweeping generalizations about why everyone might benefit from using these products.*

*She rambled on and fumbled to find a specific product to hold up to show the audience. About eight minutes into her fifteen-minute presentation, it was ap-parent that she had lost the audience. Side conversations began, phones came out. The host let her continue for a few minutes, then politely let her know her time was (prematurely) up.*

*She rushed to present one more product line, but it was too late. Few, if any, audience members were interested in listening. She received polite applause and sat down wondering what she could have done differently.*

Emily worked hard to prepare her presentation, but she was not prepared to deliver it effectively.

## It's Show Time

Time to present! You've done all the necessary things to get ready for your presentation:

- You have a clear objective
- You've done your homework about your audience
- Your presentation has a strong structure
- You've incorporated an engaging, memorable story
- Your content is compelling
- Your deck design is persuasive

But you're not quite ready... yet.

You need to prepare *yourself*, both psychologically through rehearsal and practically by checking over your materials and venue. Then you need to deliver your presentation dynamically, picking up signals from your audience and adapting your style on the fly to keep them with you on your journey.

This chapter outlines the steps that many of our clients overlook or don't spend enough time working through to ensure the presentation will accomplish its objective, along with key skills to apply while presenting to keep the audience engaged.

# Prepare yourself to present

Have you ever noticed that almost all professionals practice and warm up before engaging in their craft? Golfers hit the driving range, singers warm up their voices, gymnasts stretch. You need to prepare, too. Here are some basic ways to warm up like the pros.

## Practice your natural stance

When we're facilitating a presentation skills workshop, this is the time that we get people out of their seats to "try on" their stance. Go ahead. Stand up. Now loosen up by rolling your shoulders backward several times. Then forward. Turn your head to the left, then the right. Roll your head right, back, left and forward several times. Grab your left wrist with your right hand and raise your arms over your head. Gently pull your wrist. Change hands and repeat. Now grab your left wrist with your right hand behind your back. Gently raise your arms.

Drop your arms to your sides. Shake out your arms for several seconds and then let them fall naturally to your sides. This arm and hand placement is likely your most comfortable position.

Next, take several steps while standing in place. Shake out each foot. Then place your feet shoulder-width apart. Notice where your head, hips and shoulders line up with your ankles. For most people, the most comfortable stance for presenting is when your head is lined up in the center, with the shoulders and hips aligned over your ankles.

This is your most natural stance, your home base. You are perfectly lined up with your hands comfortably at your sides. Remain standing this way for several minutes, getting comfortable with this look and feel. From this stance, you can easily make natural movements with your arms and hands. You can take a step or two forward or sideways and then re-establish your stance.

*Become comfortable with your natural stance*

Why go to all this trouble? You've known how to stand since you were a year old, right?

But standing in front of an audience is not just standing. Having a nervous, off-balance stance is distracting and draining. Your body sends you signals that it is not comfortable, so you shift to adjust. This accentuates your nervousness, and the shifting continues.

Nervous presenters tend to have a more closed body position: shoulders rounded forward, upper body leaning off center, hands awkwardly placed either in the fig leaf position or the military at-ease stance. Not only does this look awkward, the audience can sense the nervousness. This stance can also get in the way of breathing easily, which compounds your body's problems and can actually trigger panic or lead to hyperventilating.

Using a natural stance with open body language allows you to stand comfortably and naturally and convey confidence. This adds to your credibility and enables your audience to connect with what you are saying.

Take the time to find your stance. Practice this every day until you are comfortable and are no longer having to think about what to do with your body.

## Warm up your voice

Professional singers know the importance of warming up their voices before performing. Professional speakers do, too.

Stand up and start by working the muscles in your face. Try on a big, exaggerated smile. Then frown and scowl. Go back and forth a few times. Next, yawn BIG. Then open your mouth, stick your tongue out and wag it back and forth. Last, put your lips together and exhale through your lips while making a *brrrrrr* sound. If you want a good laugh, do this in front of a mirror!

The next step is working on your vocal chords. Take a deep breath and slowly exhale while vocalizing a hum until you are out of breath. Pay attention to the vibration on your lips and your vocal chords.

Next, try one of these simple tongue twisters to work on your articulation:

*The tip of the tongue, the lips and the teeth.*
*Peter Piper picked a peck of pickled peppers.*
*She sells sea shells by the sea shore.*

As you say the phrase, articulate each word. Say the phrase a second time and say it loudly. Then say it softly. Then try saying it going from loud to soft and back to loud. If you enjoy singing, go ahead and sing out loud. This will help to relax your throat muscles. A side benefit is that we tend to breathe more deeply when singing, which can be calming.

## Breathe

A typical nervous reaction is to breathe poorly, taking quick, shallow breaths. This can actually cause you to lose focus, increase anxiety and tension and can make others uncomfortable.

Practicing good breathing helps to reduce nervousness and anxiety, provides a sense of calm and energy and can help you gain more voice control.

About 15 minutes before I present, I like to use the deep breathing techniques I learned in yoga. Here is the pattern that works for me:

1. Breathe in deeply through your nose while counting from one to four. Breathe in calmness.

2. Exhale slowly through your nose while counting down from four to one. Exhale anxiety.

3. Place your hand on your belly and visualize a wave rising and falling as you breathe.

4. Repeat several times while not engaging in any specific thought.

I usually do this while standing, with closed eyes. I can often feel my heart rate go down. When I open my eyes, I often feel a sense of peace and calm. Give it a try.

## Smile

It turns out that smiling has incredible benefits for you and for your audience. Every time you smile your brain releases neuropeptides that fight off stress. Dopamine, endorphins and serotonin get to work to relax your body and lower your heart rate.

Photo courtesy of EmbraceConsulting.biz
*Your natural, sincere smile benefits you and your audience*

When you smile, "you're viewed as attractive, reliable, relaxed and sincere."[1] Audiences respond positively, often feeling more at ease and less critical. Smiling is actually contagious. When you smile, others respond in kind in an unconscious automatic response. Seeing your audience responding to you with smiles can then have the effect of helping you to relax and feel more comfortable.

So, practice your smile in your preparation time. And make it a habit to make eye contact with audience members and smile genuinely when it's appropriate during your presentation.

## Visualize

As part of your presentation preparation, take advantage of a technique used by professional athletes. Have you ever seen downhill skiers standing at the top of the hill with closed eyes, moving their arms and legs and twisting at the waist while performing what seems to be an unusual pre-race dance? They are actually visualizing how they will maneuver the course. You can do the same thing.

According to *Psychology Today*, "Brain studies reveal that thoughts produce the same mental instructions as actions. Mental imagery impacts many cognitive processes in the brain: motor control, attention, perception, planning and memory. So, the brain is getting trained for actual performance during visualization. It's been found that mental practices can enhance motivation, increase confidence and self-efficacy, improve motor performance, prime your brain for success, and increase states of flow."[2]

After you've done your deep breathing routine, close your eyes and visualize yourself standing confidently, comfortably in front of your audience. See your smile.

Imagine the smiles on the faces in your audience. Imagine the engaged expressions as your audience asks thoughtful questions. Then take in the applause you will receive for a great presentation.

## Practice positive affirmation

Another technique to help you program yourself for success is positive affirmation. An affirmation is a positive statement to help you overcome negative thoughts by replacing them with positive thoughts. Negative thoughts and fears can sabotage presentation performance. Instead, harness the power of the self-fulfilling prophecy by substituting positive for negative.

Start by writing down your presentation affirmation. This can be as simple as...

*I present confidently and comfortably*

*I am passionate about sharing my knowledge and making a difference in others' lives*

*I am a subject matter expert on X and present with enthusiasm*

*I am a presenter who inspires others*

Your affirmation needs to be positive, achievable and credible. Write this in the present tense as if it is already happening. Post your handwritten affirmation where you will see it regularly and will be reminded to repeat it throughout the day.

As you prepare to present, repeat this in your head several times. Then, say your affirmation out loud, with emotion and commitment.

## Focus on empowering self-questions

One more technique to ensure you keep negative thoughts at bay is to focus on empowering self-questions, such as:

*What is the best possible outcome following this presentation?*

*How can I reach each audience member?*

*How can I make a difference in the lives of my audience?*

## Remind yourself of your objective

Your very first step in developing your presentation was establishing your presentation objective. This is your driving force, what you want to accomplish. Your objective includes *why* you want to influence your audience. Your delivery is how you will do so.

So, before you step in front of your audience, remind yourself of your *why*. Be laser focused on why you want to influence them.

## Practice, practice, practice

*There is no glory in practice, but without practice, there is no glory.* I'm not sure who said this, but I completely agree. Practicing your presentation is what will help you to deliver convincingly and influentially. Your goal is to become completely comfortable with your content, so that you appear comfortable and have natural body language on stage. Here are some tips for practicing that will increase your professionalism and minimize your anxiety.

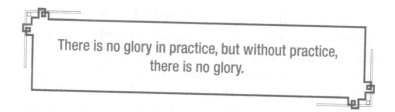

There is no glory in practice, but without practice, there is no glory.

## Really practice

As one of my favorite mentors used to tell me, "Practice makes perfect only what you practice." Don't just go through your slides and imagine what you will say with each slide. Really practice. That includes using the projector and clicker, standing up in front of the room and speaking out loud. Going through your presentation at your desk and imagining your presentation does not provide the same experience as hearing your voice, experimenting with how you will use your voice, practicing how you will move and becoming comfortable with equipment such as the wireless slide clicker and laser.

## Practice with feedback

An easy way to get feedback on your presentation is to video record your rehearsal. Set up your smart phone or tablet and hit record. Then, as painful as it might be, watch your presentation and take notes. What did you do well? What do you need to tweak? What can you eliminate? Then repeat the process. Doing this several times will help you to perfect your delivery and increase your comfort. And the more comfortable you are with your presentation, the more you will connect with your audience.

To get live feedback, ask friends, family members or colleagues to help you by attending a practice presentation. Set the stage by telling them in advance who your audience will be that you want them to sit in for. Also, let them know that you are going to ask for their feedback. Then present just as you would for your real audience.

When finished, ask for their specific feedback on your introduction, content, delivery, deck design and closing. Ask them what the objective of the presentation is. And then ask them what points they remember or how they would summarize your presentation. Their responses will point out any adjustments you need to make in content and delivery.

## Practice using technology

Practice using Presenter View so that you can casually and naturally glance at your laptop to see what your next slide will be. For many people, this feature is the ultimate safety net. Not only will you not be surprised or stand wondering what's next, you can add the key point for each slide as a reminder in the notes section.

*A note about notes in slide decks*: Too often we see people adding large blocks of text as notes so they "won't forget something." This often backfires. These notes are small and not easily read at a glance and from a distance. And if you have many notes, you will be visibly focusing on the laptop and obviously distracted from your audience.

If you need to use the notes section, keep your notes brief and limit the notes to the key idea for that slide.

*A note about using laser pointers*: I have rarely seen presenters use a laser pointer effectively. Too often the laser is actually distracting, as the presenter nervously moves the red dot around the screen in a jerky, migraine-inducing fashion. If you feel you need to use a laser pointer, practice using it. Move it as little as possible around the screen. Highlight what's important and turn it off.

A fair number of people cannot easily see the tiny laser dot on the screen. Another reason to avoid using a laser pointer is that to use it, you must turn your back on your audience. That's not the side of you the audience came to see!

The primary reason presenters use a laser pointer is because the slide is overstuffed. The remedy for this is to create slides that don't require you to use a pointer for the audience to get the point.

If you present frequently, we suggest that you purchase a remote slide clicker. This is presentation insurance. It's never fun to arrive for a presentation and discover that there is no clicker, or that the clicker provided doesn't work. You are then trapped in close proximity to your laptop to advance your slides.

Finally, always carry fresh spare batteries for these tools. Batteries always seem to die at the most inopportune time, so be prepared.

## Practice your introduction...a lot

Your introduction is critical. You must break mental pre-occupation, capture attention, establish your credibility and convince your audience to stay tuned. Yet starting out is often the hardest part. We suggest you practice your introduction a lot... to the point where it is almost second nature. Go over it again and again until you are confident that when you stand up to begin your presentation, you know the introduction will do all it needs to do. You don't need to memorize it. In fact, memorizing your introduction word for word can be too much pressure and may leave you lost if you lose your place.

Instead, be comfortable with what you want to include in the introduction and how you will link the main points. And don't forget to use your smile!

## Prepare your materials and venue

### Extra presentation precautions

Always bring your presentation deck on a USB thumb drive. If your laptop has technical difficulties, you can borrow a laptop, load your presentation and continue. Also, print copies of your slides in case the Presenter View feature doesn't work.

### Take control of your stage

Whenever possible, check out your presentation area in advance. Knowing your venue set-up in advance can prevent nervousness and helps to avoid last minute issues which can derail your mental focus right before you present.

Test your laptop with the available equipment. Start with the projector. Check the quality of the visual image of your slides on the screen. If there are lights over the screen, see if they can be turned off or dimmed so that they don't wash out your slides.

The preferred projector arrangement is one which is attached to the ceiling. When the projector sits on a table, you will disrupt the display each time you walk from one side of the room to the other. If you are stuck with a table-based projector, the best solution is to re-arrange the room by moving the screen to the left-front corner of the room if you're right-handed, or the right-front corner if left-handed. This enables you to use your dominant hand to naturally make gestures toward the screen. By using the corner of the room for display, you command the center of attention in the front of the room.

Test the remote slide clicker, and if you're using video with sound, be sure to check out the sound in the room. Your laptop speakers will not enable people to hear what you're presenting in a large room. Most plug-in computer speakers are also fairly weak. If you're going to use audio, make sure the presentation room has good built-in speakers, or bring your own powerful Bluetooth speaker. As part of your pre-test, make sure your speaker is fully charged and you are linked to your laptop.

If there are power cords in the area where you will be presenting, have them taped down so you won't trip.

## Presentation day prep

On the day of your presentation, your success relies on you being physically prepared to present.

- Arrive well-rested

- Eat a light, nutritious meal

- Be sure you are hydrated, and bring water with you

- Don't over caffeinate

- Dress for success: wear professional clothes that are comfortable and a bit dressier than the clothes your audience is likely to wear

Arrive well in advance of your presentation time. Get your equipment set up and make any room adjustments that are needed. Move chairs and tables as necessary to ensure everyone has a seat and can see you and the screen. Always plug in your laptop to direct power. Do not rely on your computer's battery even when you think it's fully charged.

As people begin to arrive, greet them and introduce yourself to those you don't know. Get to know a little about what your guests want to learn. See your audience as people who share your worries, frustrations and anxieties. Making these connections will allow you to spot a few friendly faces in the audience. You can also call on your new "friends" during the presentation to create connections with the audience. When audience members see that you are engaging with them, they tend to pay closer attention.

## Deliver with impact

Delivering your presentation is about sharing your knowledge by harnessing the power of your voice, using positive body language and reading the body language in the audience. Presenters who deliver confidently are more likely to be trusted by the audience, which leads to increased influence.

## Harness the power of your voice

Think of your voice as you might think of a musical instrument. Your presentation is the musical score, and you must make the music come alive. Use your voice to let your passion and enthusiasm for your topic come through. There are five vocal delivery tools you can use to influence your audience. We call them *The Five Ps*.

## Pronunciation

Pronunciation is the way a word is spoken, placing emphasis on appropriate syllables. In our decades-long experience working with life science companies, we've learned the importance of practicing pronunciation for long, polysyllabic words. If your presentation contains hard-to-pronounce terms, speak them slowly and explain their meaning if they're likely to be new to your audience.

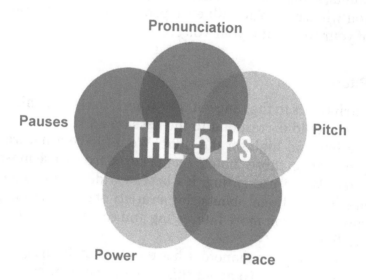

Articulation is a bit different than pronunciation. Articulation is saying words clearly and audibly. Articulate presenters do not mumble or drop the endings from words. Dropping the 'g' from words ending in -ing is fine in casual conversation (*we're goin' to start at noon*), but this makes you sound unprofessional when presenting.

Another aspect of pronunciation is what words you emphasize in a sentence. Consider how different this sentence is when emphasizing the bold words:

*I* said he was a scoundrel
I **said** he was a scoundrel
I said **he** was a scoundrel
I said he **was** a scoundrel
I said he was a **scoundrel**

Strong presenters practice pronunciation, articulation and emphasis. Have some fun with this. For important points, statements or conclusions, experiment with how you will say it. You influence people with the emotion of your words and your voice.

## Pitch

Pitch refers to the range of your voice, from low to high. Pitch could correspond to the keys on a piano: low on the left and high on the right. We all have a natural pitch range, those "notes" on the keyboard we use most often. When presenting, it's best to widen your range and be intentional about using a variety of pitches. Doing this makes you more interesting and can enhance your credibility.

Speaking in a monotone has the effect of disengaging your audience. To avoid this, expand your pitch and practice mixing it up.

## Pace

Almost as boring as a monotone is a mono-pace. Using the same delivery pace throughout your presentation has the effect of lulling the audience to sleep. Speaking fast can be energizing unless it's done for too long. Likewise, a slower pace can be great for emphasizing certain points. But speaking slowly for too long allows the audience time to wander mentally. Know your normal pace and vary it to keep the audience engaged.

## Power

Power refers to the volume of your voice. Like pace, varying your power can be an effective way to influence the emotions of the audience. Speaking loudly definitely gets attention, but it can be tiresome for the audience and for you. Speaking softly can be equally effective for emphasizing key points.

The key to being an engaging presenter is vocal variety. And when you think you've made a big adjustment in your vocal variety, you've probably only altered the power a bit. Record yourself rehearsing your presentation and deliberately work on vocal variety. Before reviewing that recording, do it again and plan on doubling the range of your volume. Then compare the two recordings. The second one is usually the more interesting.

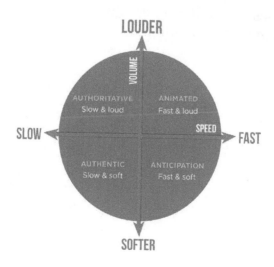

## Pauses

The last of the *Five Ps* is to pause. Pausing has many benefits for you and your audience. Benefits for you include:

- Adding emphasis... letting your last words sink in
- Time to formulate what you'll say next
- Opportunity to breathe deeply
- Time to read your audience

The audience benefits of an intentional, well-placed pause include:

- Time to take in and process what you've said
- Opportunity to connect the dots of your key points
- Time to come up with well thought out questions

Pauses are your friends. Embrace them and plan them in your presentation.

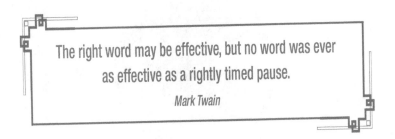

The right word may be effective, but no word was ever as effective as a rightly timed pause.

*Mark Twain*

# Use positive body language

Your audience pays as much attention to how you present as they do to what you say. They are constantly reading your body language. So be intentional and practice positive body language.

## Be aware of your gesture zone

The most comfortable range of motion for natural gestures while presenting is the area from your shoulders to your waist and as broad as your extended elbows. It's okay to gesture outside of this zone for extreme emphasis. But staying outside the zone for too long may cause you to be perceived as extreme and even unpolished.

*Practice your gestures so they feel comfortable and appear natural*

Gestures include your head as well as the arms and hands. Leaning forward demonstrates interest.

Be aware of your facial expressions. Your eyes, eyebrows and mouth help deliver your messages. Match your facial expressions to the point you're making. For example, saying, "I was surprised by these results" might be matched with a facial expression that has wide eyes, raised eyebrows and a cocked head. But don't overdo it: you'll appear unnatural and may diminish your credibility.

Nodding and smiling relaxes you and your audience. As appropriate, mirror the level of formality you see in the audience.

When not gesturing, practice being comfortable with your hands at your sides in your natural stance. Postures to avoid include:

- Crossed arms – possibly perceived as defensive, very closed or unapproachable

- Hand on hips – too authoritative, possibly seen as being critical or judgmental

- Hands in pockets – may appear too casual or uninterested in what you're doing

- Fig leaf (hands clasped in front below the waist) – displays nervousness, lack of confidence, timidity

- Hands clasped behind back – can be perceived as rigid or too formal

And while we're on the topic of what not to do, avoid fiddling with things in your pocket. To prevent yourself from doing this inadvertently, empty your pockets before you take the stage.

## Be intentional about movement

Presenters typically fall into one of two opposing movement styles: frozen in place or frenetic pacing. The following tips will help both types develop a more comfortable, natural, believable style.

Move comfortably and purposefully. We recommend the *move–plant–deliver* approach. Move to a new position. Plant your feet shoulder width apart. Then deliver the next part of your presentation. Stay in this place for a few minutes. Then, when you make the next transition in your presentation, repeat this process.

# MOVE - PLANT - DELIVER

- Once you become comfortable with this technique, you can add transition statements as you move.

- Use different parts of the room to make different points. You can then move back to that part of the room to reference the earlier point. Doing this creates mental markers for the audience.

- Never turn your back to the audience. We see inexperienced presenters doing this frequently. Have your laptop between you and the audience so you can glance at it vs. looking back at the screen.

- Never touch the screen. This can cause the screen to move, distorting the image, which can distract your audience.

- Move closer to and then away from the audience to create different focal points. This heightens interest and keeps the audience alert.

- If possible, don't stand behind a lectern. This creates a barrier between the presenter and the audience and can make the presenter seem cold, formal or less convincing.

- If you are in a large room, arrange for a wireless microphone so you will be heard by those in the back row, and you are not tethered with a cord.

- Don't block the image from the projector. If the projector is not ceiling mounted, present in the space behind or to the side of the projector.

- Also, avoid standing such that the image is projecting on your body or into your eyes. We've seen presenters squinting at the audience from standing with the projector light shining in their eyes. This distracts the audience and diminishes credibility.

## Eliminate filler words

Why do filler words such as um, so, and uh creep into our presentations? Because we're buying time to prepare the next sentence. The best way to eliminate these words is to be intentional about finishing your sentence. That's right—finish your sentence. Period. Pause. Start the next sentence.

## Make positive eye contact

Making positive eye contact is one of your most powerful tools for influence. Eye contact demonstrates that you are interested in your audience. It helps you build rapport and connect emotionally. It also conveys confidence, enhances your credibility and increases your believability. Make soft eye contact for approximately three to five seconds. This will help you monitor audience engagement and prevent sweeping, nervous eye movement.

# Read audience body language

To increase your level of influence, develop a sixth sense for reading your audience. The body language you observe will give you information on how well you are reaching the audience.

Assess the interaction of the people in the audience before you begin. Are they friendly, chatting, lively? If so, you are more likely to be successful in engaging and involving them during your presentation.

If the audience is not interacting, you will need to make them feel comfortable with you and with one another by showing them that they will benefit from paying attention. Let them know what's in it for them. Be warm and encouraging with your tone. When you see cues like positive eye contact, smiles and open body language, you'll know the audience has started to relax and will be easier to engage.

As you present, use these insights to adjust your delivery to increase audience engagement:

**Engaged behaviors: positive eye contact, leaning forward or sitting upright, taking notes, nodding, raised eyebrows, generally open and relaxed posture**

When you notice engaged behaviors, determine what you said that caused this. Tap into this engagement by doing more of what triggered their behavior. Fast nodding usually indicates acceptance of what you're saying. Slow nodding demonstrates interest and wanting to know more.

*Pensive and interested behaviors*: eyes narrowed, head tilted to side, hand touching face

These behaviors let you know the audience is taking in what you've shared. Continue to provide information that moves them from pensive to accepting.

*Neutral behaviors*: blank expression, sitting upright

This is often what you will see at the beginning of your presentation as the audience reads you and determines whether you are credible and believable. Neutral is not bad.

*Bored/disengaged behaviors*: using phones, staring off, doodling, no eye contact, slumping, whispering, vacant looks, sleeping

Move closer to the audience, change your pace, adjust your power. Ask a question directly to one audience member. These tactics let the audience know that you're interested in getting their attention.

## Impatient behaviors: fast nodding ("I get it...keep going already!"), restlessness, turning away

Move on! Even if you have more to say on this point, assume that the audience is done with it. Better to move on than to lose the audience.

## Confused behaviors: head cocked to the side, furrowed brow, one raised eyebrow, mouth skewed to one side

Try explaining your point a different way. You can also ask a question to determine what is causing confusion. For example, "How might you envision using this concept/tool/idea in your world?" It's best to ask this directly to one individual. If you ask this as a general question, the natural tendency for confused people will be to avoid eye contact to dodge the question. By asking the question to one individual, that person can attempt to answer or admit that they're lost. This gives you information on how to adjust course to clarify your point, remove confusion and get back on track.

## Disapproving behaviors: crossed arms and/or legs, frowning, side conversations, lack of eye contact, belligerent questions, tight-lipped expression, loud exhaling

Be honest. Let your audience know you're reading their behavior and ask for their input. For example, "I'm sensing that some of you are not on board with what I've shared. Tell me how you see this." Listen attentively.

Be prepared to respond positively, appreciatively and non-defensively. Thank those who respond and use their input to re-frame your point and incorporate their views.

Time of day can affect audience behavior. Your audience may have more energy in the morning compared to just after lunch. Adjust your pace, power and energy as needed. Your goal is to assess the majority of the audience and adjust delivery as needed.

## Leverage your influence via Q&A

After you've finished the presentation, you're still not finished influencing your audience. Answering questions is another opportunity for you to reinforce your presentation objective. Done well, the Q&A period can be a golden influence opportunity. Here's how to leverage this time to win the audience over to your point of view.

First, graciously invite and encourage questions. Make it comfortable for people to respond by saying something like, "I know we've covered a lot of ground. You may still be processing some of what I said; I know I often am after a presentation like this. I'm happy to respond to questions, and if you have a question, it's highly probable that others do, too. The answers I can provide to your questions will most likely benefit them as well."

When a question is asked, repeat or paraphrase the question while maintaining eye contact with the questioner. This ensures everyone hears the question. It also makes sure the questioner feels understood and valued. This step also makes sure you understand the question. And perhaps the hidden benefit from this step is that it buys you time to formulate a response.

If you didn't understand the question, politely ask for clarification.

When responding to the question, make eye contact with the questioner and use her name if you know it. As you respond, make eye contact with others, too. This creates a sense of inclusion.

Be sure you answer the question that was asked, not what you wish had been asked. After providing your answer, provide the logic behind your response. Then, provide an example. If possible, provide an example that supports the points you are attempting to influence. To really leverage your influence, tie your response back to your presentation objective if appropriate.

If you don't know the answer to a question, do not guess or bluff. Make a note of the question and promise to get back to the questioner. Then do that promptly.

If no questions are asked and there are points you want to reiterate, you can offer those up as questions usually asked. Then proceed to provide the answer and the compelling logic that supports the answer.

Keep your answers concise and on point. This isn't the time to start a second presentation. Remember: the audience has graciously gifted you with their time and attention. Don't abuse the privilege!

Wrap up the Q&A session by briefly restating your conclusion and/or call to action, focusing on why this is beneficial for the audience. Keep the focus on what's in it for them. Make sure this conclusion is compelling and memorable.

# Final notes

Always strive to finish on time or maybe even a bit early. This demonstrates respect for the audience and distinguishes you as a presenter of integrity.

If there is a commitment or a decision you are seeking from the audience, be direct. Make it clear what you want and how you will know they are committed.

Be complete in covering all the points necessary to achieve your presentation objective. It's often compelling to leave the audience wanting more so that they will want to engage in a personal conversation with you after you finish.

Then, be prepared to follow up. Sometimes your work is not done when the presentation ends. To achieve your influence objective, you may need to follow up and be persistent with key decision makers in the audience.

You started the presentation journey to accomplish a specific influence objective. Assess your success by reviewing your presentation after you've concluded. Did you get the response you anticipated? Did the audience commit to your request or call to action? If you are uncertain, reach out to thought leaders in the audience and ask for their feedback on your presentation. Determine their willingness to commit to your cause or join you in next steps. Then, continue to follow up.

## Summary of Key Ideas

- Serious professionals warm up before they perform, compete or present. You need to warm up, too. Here is your warm-up checklist:

  - Practice your natural stance

  - Warm up your voice

  - Breathe

  - Smile

  - Visualize

  - Practice positive affirmation

  - Focus on empowering self-questions

  - Remind yourself of your objective

- Practice your presentation using technology and get feedback. Repeat!

- Prepare your materials and your venue. Always have your presentation on a thumb drive in case of technical problems with your computer. Print out and bring a copy of your slides in case presenter view does not work on the laptop you're using.

- Take control of your stage. Check that all technology is working. Make sure the room is arranged so that you are visible to everyone in the audience. If necessary, move tables and chairs to create the optimal environment. If there are power cords where you will be presenting, ask to have those taped down.

- Arrive early for your presentation. Be sure you are well rested, hydrated, not hungry and not overly caffeinated. Choose appropriate clothes that are comfortable and enhance your confidence. Greet your audience members as they arrive. Introduce yourself to those whom you do not know.

- Harness the power of your voice by varying the Five Ps: pronunciation, pitch, pace, pauses and power.

- Use positive body language. Videotape your practice presentation and identify behaviors that do and don't work for you. Modify those and practice some more. Become comfortable using a variety of gestures inside the gesture zone.

- Avoid nervous pacing by practicing the *move–plant–deliver* technique.

- Eliminate filler words by being intentional about finishing your sentences.

- To increase your influence, learn to read audience body language so you can adapt appropriately as you present.

- Leverage your influence during the question and answer period by making a personal connection with those who ask questions. Make eye contact, use the questioner's name if you know it, repeat the question, respond. Then relate your response back to your presentation objective if appropriate.

- When concluding, take your audience back to your influence objective. Be direct about asking for a commitment or a decision if either is needed.

- Always conclude on time or a bit early. Never overstay your welcome by taking more time than you were granted.

## Put This to Work

1. Create your own presentation checklists for your presentation warm-up routine, materials and venue

2. Take a video of your presentation. Then review it and assess the items below on a scale of 1 (not great) to 10 (you're a pro)

|  | SCORE |
|---|---|
| *Vocal Variety* |  |
| Pronunciation variation |  |
| Pitch alteration |  |
| Pace changes |  |
| Power variation |  |
| Pause usage |  |
| Body Language |  |
| Natural gestures in the "gesture zone" |  |
| Intentional movement: *move–plant– deliver* |  |
| Avoidance of filler words |  |
| *Influence* |  |
| Your conclusion takes the audience to the influence objective |  |
| You asked for a specific commitment or decision |  |

## Resources

[1] Riggio, Ronald E. Ph.D. "There's Magic in Your Smile." *Psychology Today*, June 25, 2012.

[2] Adams, A.J. "Seeing is Believing: The Power of Visualization." PsychologyToday.com December 3, 2009.

# CHAPTER 8

# **Keep Improving**

After you've finished a presentation, it might be tempting to close the file with a sigh of relief that you don't have to think about it again for a while. But this is the best time to do any necessary follow up to make sure your influence objective sticks, as well as to review and improve upon your presentation for next time. No matter how compelling your presentation is in the moment, there are some concrete steps you can take after it's over to reinforce your message.

## Influence doesn't end at the last slide

The presentation is over, but the influence process may not be. If your influence objective required a commitment, a decision, support or a change of behavior, you will need to follow up. Be direct with your influence targets. Ask for the support or change. Be sure to focus on the why of your presentation as you follow up. And be clear about the benefit others will receive as a result of committing to your request.

## Use strategies for continuous improvement

Take the time to review your presentation within a day or two. Use a Plus/Delta approach. Make two columns. On the left, what were the pluses of your presentation? Be specific about what worked. On the right, identify the deltas or things you feel you would like to change on the right. If you have a video of your presentation, review it for both content and delivery. Go through your presentation point by point, slide by slide. What worked? What needs improvement? Be specific.

You can also ask for feedback from a few people who attended your presentation. Let them know that you are seeking both positive and constructive feedback so that you can improve your skills.

Take the time to make any revisions to your deck while your review is top of mind. This will help you to lock in the things you've learned. And if you will be giving this presentation in the future, your prep time will be shorter with your revised deck.

## Be intentional about improving

Becoming a skilled 21st century presenter will take time and experience. Seek opportunities to present. Get out of your comfort zone and present on a variety of topics. The more you present, the more your confidence and competence will grow.

Attend a variety of presentations including those within your company and industry and those from other industries. Check out presentations on line, too. Watch these presentations with the intention of learning from others. Take away one or two ideas from each. You may even want to keep a presentations notebook to capture what you're learning. Then before you begin creating your next presentation, review your notes and include the best practices you've gathered.

## Final thoughts

I hope that you will be bold and disciplined in developing your presentation skills. Boldly try the tools, tips and techniques in this book. And be disciplined in practicing and in incorporating the feedback you receive.

Remember: You are taking your audience on a journey with a specific destination. When you take the time to understand the needs of your audience, they will happily go with you on that journey. Your audience will appreciate your application of the tools in this book. Your presentations will be clear and concise. Adding your powerful delivery will lead to compelling and influential presentations. I hope you and your audience enjoy the journey!

# ABOUT THE AUTHOR

Susan Garrity Bish is passionate about helping people learn, apply and benefit from communication and management skills that change careers. She is the co-founder and managing partner of Bottom Line Technologies, a consulting firm that has played a leading role in equipping global leaders for success. When she is not focused on making a difference in others' lives, she can be found in North Carolina on Lake Norman with her husband, Myron, and BFF (Best Furry Friend), Blaze.

# You've read the book.
## Are you ready to put *Clear, Concise & Compelling* to work?

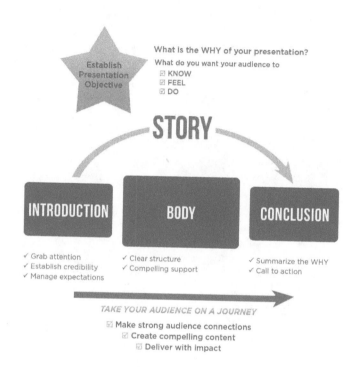

## Here are two ways to help yourself and others:

*1* Schedule a *Clear, Concise & Compelling* workshop

*2* Become a certified instructor for *Clear, Concise & Compelling*

**Check out details on our website**
**www.BottomLineTechnologiesNC.com**

CPSIA information can be obtained
at www.ICGtesting.com
Printed in the USA
FFHW011741041119
55888947-61768FF